# The Recorder
## in the
## Nineteenth Century

# The
# Recorder
## in the
# Nineteenth
# Century

DOUGLAS MACMILLAN

ISBN 978-1-904846-33-8
First Published 2008

© Douglas Macmillan 2008

All rights reserved. No part of this publication may be reproduced, stored in a retrieval system, or transmitted in any form or by any means, electronic, mechanical, photocopying, recording or otherwise, without the prior permission in writing of the Publisher.

Designed by David Miller
Printed by Lightning Source UK
Published by Ruxbury Publications
Scout Bottom Farm
Mytholmroyd
West Yorkshire
HX7 5JS (GB)

**CONTENTS**

| | | |
|---|---|---|
| Chapter I | Introduction<br>*The recorder, the csakan and the flageolet* | 9 |
| Chapter II | The Decline of the Recorder in the eighteenth Century | 15 |
| Chapter III | Inventory of Recorders 1800-1905 | 25 |
| Chapter IV | The Recorders discussed | 101 |
| Chapter V | The Berchtesgadner Fleitl | 113 |
| Chapter VI | Music for the Recorder<br>*Music, treatises and use of the recorder* | 121 |
| Chapter VII | The Recorder in Art and Literature | 133 |
| Chapter VIII | Introduction to the Recorder Revival | 139 |
| Chapter IX | The Revival of the Recorder<br>*England, France, Germany and Belgium* | 147 |
| Chapter X | Obsolete and Eclipsed? | 177 |
| Bibliography | | 181 |
| Index | | 183 |

## PREFACE

In the early 1980s I cast my eyes on a large recorder, which at the time reposed upon Carl Dolmetsch's kitchen table. Dr Dolmetsch – perceiving my immediate interest – related that the instrument was a voice flute bearing the stamp METZLER/LONDON/105. WARDOUR ST. and suggested that the instrument may be of nineteenth-century origin: I now realize that this brief encounter over a cup of coffee kindled my interest in an unexplored dark age of the recorder's history. A period of research led to my being awarded the Fellowship of Trinity College, London, for a thesis entitled *The Recorder in the late eighteenth and early nineteenth Centuries* wherein I noted the continued manufacture of recorders (albeit in tiny numbers) well into the second half of the nineteenth century and commented that 'The century which saw the virtual end of the recorder also witnessed the earliest dawn of its new beginning'.

My interest in the subject then lay dormant until I attended a lecture-recital in the millennial year by Nikolaj Tarasov on *The Development of the Recorder from 1750 until the Present*: re-enthused, I resumed my research and in 2005 was awarded a PhD by the University of Surrey (England) for my thesis *The Recorder 1800-1905*. The thesis forms the backbone of the present book: some rather 'dry' academic material has been omitted, further recorders have been added to the inventory and speculative hypotheses have been revised in the light of further research.

A study of the organology of the recorder in the nineteenth century forms the core of the work, for without the instruments there would be no history to relate. The decline of the recorder in the late eighteenth century is discussed in order to place the nineteenth-century recorder within an historical context and further chapters explore music for, and use of, the recorder in the nineteenth century and discuss its appearance in iconography and literature. A brief examination of the philosophy of the early music revival is given prior to the second principal topic, the revival of the recorder, a phenomenon which arose spontaneously in several European countries in the final quarter of the nineteenth century.

Although the title 'The recorder in the nineteenth century' suggests that the study should end in 1899, I have chosen to extend the nineteenth century for a further few years (!) until 1905: not only are these additional years are of considerable interest in the saga of the recorder revival in England but also the year 1905 is of especial significance for in June of that year Arnold Dolmetsch (a name irrevocably linked with the recorder) purchased his celebrated Bressan alto recorder.

Many scholarly musicians have encouraged and contributed to the project, and to all these – although too numerous to mention by name – I express my gratitude. In particular, I wish to thank my doctoral supervisor Professor Emeritus Sebastian Forbes, Dr Florence

Gétreau, Dr Kurt Birsak, Nicolaj Tarasov, Ture Bergstrøm, and Bernardt Oeggl. Rachel Barnes has been a staunch ally throughout the project, and I also acknowledge with gratitude the help afforded by the late Dr Hélène la Rue, whose untimely death in the summer of this year has been deeply felt by many organologists. If this small book goes some way to perpetuate the memory of a gracious friend, I shall be proud.

At the end of the list – yet foremost in her unique importance – comes my wife Emma, herself a musician. Not only is she a brilliant and sensitive harpsichordist but has often acted as an unpaid research assistant, culling obscurities from the depths of the internet and has provoked, criticized, encouraged (and, at times, applauded) my work and has endured the long hours of separation from domesticity which a research project inevitably demands. I can only express my deepest gratitude.

Finally, it is my wish to dedicate this study of the recorder in the nineteenth century to the memory of the late Dr Carl Dolmetsch, musician, scholar and dear friend – 'Papa'.

Douglas MacMillan

2007

*The Recorder In The Nineteenth Century*

# CHAPTER I

## INTRODUCTION

### THE RECORDER, THE CSAKAN AND THE FLAGEOLET

The recorder reached the zenith of its popularity in the sixteenth, seventeenth and eighteenth centuries, declining in use as the late baroque gave way to the classical period. Textbooks of musical history relate that it then lay dormant during the nineteenth century, only to be revived in the early twentieth century by such pioneers of the early music movement as Arnold Dolmetsch. Recent research, however, has demonstrated that recorders continued to be made (although in very small numbers) throughout the nineteenth century and that its revival began spontaneously across Europe in the latter years of that century.

This book tells the story of the recorder between 1800 (when it had disappeared from mainstream musical practice) up to the year when Arnold Dolmetsch purchased an alto recorder made by Bressan, writing that day in his diary *Cela me sera très utile* (that will be very useful to me). It is necessary to define the nature of the recorder, and to distinguish it from a number of similar instruments which were in use in the nineteenth century.

The recorder belongs to the family of duct flutes, that group of instruments wherein air is directed to the sound-producing edge (the labium of the recorder) via a duct from the player's mouth: the traditional English term 'fipple flute' is discarded, as considerable uncertainty exists as to what actually constitutes a 'fipple'. Included in this family are the recorder, the csakan, the flageolet, the tin whistle, and a multitude of folk instruments from around the world.

The recorder is characterized as a duct flute with seven finger holes and one thumb hole: it has a contracting conical bore from the head to the foot of the instrument and is usually built in three pieces (occasionally one [especially in the renaissance], two, or four). Most small and medium-sized recorders are keyless, but keys are often found on the larger instruments (especially bassets and basses). The flageolet (in its English and French forms) may be easily distinguished from the recorder, but the csakan has been a source of considerable confusion in studying the recorder in the nineteenth century, both with regard to its terminology and its putative role as the so-called 'romantic recorder'. The csakan, in the opinion of the present author, is a separate instrument from the recorder, coming into existence in the Austro-Hungarian Empire in the early nineteenth century and becoming obsolete by the middle of the century.

## THE CSAKAN

Like the recorder, the csakan has seven finger holes and one thumb-hole: unlike the recorder, it may be fitted with many keys, and the bore of the instrument is more cylindrical than that of the recorder. The name 'csakan' is derived from the Hungarian *csákány* meaning walking stick or cane flute and at its initial appearance in Budapest in 1807 the instrument was in the form of a cane flute: the player, Anton Heberle (fl1806-16) is credited with the invention of the instrument. Heberle's treatise, *Scala für den Ungarischen Csakan* was published in 1807 and the instrument became popular as a dilettante instrument in Vienna and its environs.

    The early csakans appeared in the form of a walking stick, the mouthpiece being in the curved handle of the instrument which was either keyless or fitted with a single key (Heberle's *Scala* shows a keyless instrument). Subsequently the csakan acquired up to thirteen keys, but the instrument never developed a consistent form: some later csakans were made without a walking-stick handle and mouthpiece and therefore blown like a recorder although on some instruments the window was placed at the back of the instrument. Later instruments had an oboe-like bell rather than a walking-stick foot. The so-called Pressburger csakans built by Schnöllnast exhibited a very small thumb-hole so that the higher octave could be obtained without 'pinching' the thumb-hole as on the recorder, whereas the Viennese pattern of csakan retained a larger thumb-hole. The oboist and csakan virtuoso Ernst Krähmer's *Csakan-Schule* of 1821 distinguished between the simple csakan (with one key) and the complex csakan(with seven). Simple csakans had a compass of two octaves, the complex versions around two octaves and a fourth (c'[notated] to f'''). Betz, in her definitive study of the instrument, lists eighty-seven surviving csakans (and describes four lost in World War II) with varying patterns of keywork, mouthpieces, foot-joints, and pitch.[1] Significant makers included Stephan Koch (Vienna, 1772-1828), Johann Ziegler (Vienna, 1792-1852) and Franz Schöllnast (Pressburg, 1775-1844). The instrument was confined to a small area of Eastern Europe centered on Vienna but it may also have been used in Russia: there is no evidence that the csakan was used in western Europe, although an organ stop marked 'csakan' appears in Lübeck.

    The majority of csakans were built in the key of A flat (lowest note a flat') although some examples exist in the keys of G, A, B flat, and C. Music for the instrument was written transposed down a minor sixth, with c' as the lowest notated note. Some 400 pieces of music were composed for the csakan between the years of 1807 and 1845, the majority of which were written for one or two csakans, sometimes with the accompaniment of guitar (in scordatura) or piano. The instrument was used in various chamber music combinations and the occasional concerto appears in the repertoire but much of csakan

---

[1] Betz, M., *Der Csakan und seine Musik*, (Tutzing: Hans Schneider 1992), pp212-229

music consisted of simple airs, variations, dances and tunes culled from current operatic favourites.

The csakan has left, in its legacy, a question mark in the controversial matter of terminology in that some pieces were written for *Csakan ou (oder) flûte douce*: this immediately poses the dilemma 'is 'flûte douce' an alternative name for the csakan or does it actually refer to a different instrument, namely the recorder?' That 'flûte douce' was (and indeed is) a name for the recorder is beyond doubt, and it may be that the educated Viennese (who would have been familiar with the French tongue) used the term for the soft-voiced csakan rather than implying the baroque-style recorder, which still existed (in very small numbers ) at that time. Much csakan music (after transposition) lies comfortably on the soprano recorder and publishers - with an eye to their livelihood – probably produced music which could be realized on either instrument. Recorder players have long been known to appropriate music intended for other instruments and there is no logical reason to suppose that the situation would have been substantially different in early nineteenth-century Vienna.

Some authors (notably Thalheimer[2] and Reyne[3]) have conceived the csakan as the 'romantic recorder' and forming an ultimate step in the evolution of the recorder. I believe it is more appropriate to consider the csakan as a romantic duct flute, for it came into being born of the walking-stick flutes of Hungarian shepherds, led a brief existence of some fifty years (during which time – as will be demonstrated in subsequent chapters – the true recorder continued in shadowy existence) before coming to a timely end, although the term 'csakan' continued in use in Germany until the 1930s, when it was applied to a variety of duct flutes, mainly intended for school or amateur use. These instruments bore no resemblance to the various forms of the Viennese csakan.

The csakan had its use in the dilettante world of the early romantics but it had disappeared from common usage long before the era of romanticism in music had ended. The period when gentlemen amused themselves (and their ladies) on walking-stick instruments had passed: the few great csakan player/composers had died, and an instrument pitched in A flat was hardly likely to endear itself to an amateur who could learn the rudiments of flute-playing and so join with other musicians without having to transpose his or her part down a minor sixth or up a major third.

## THE FLAGEOLET

The flageolet (in its several forms) is an instrument of both greater antiquity and wider distribution than the csakan, being first described in French literature of the fourteenth century: the suggestion that the flageolet was invented by Sieur Juvigny in Paris in 1591

---

[2] Thalheimer, P., 'Csakan Musik - 'eine Nische im heutigen Blockflötenrepertoire', *Tibia* 4 (2000), pp288-294
[3] Reyne, H., 'La flûte à bec romantique existe : je l'ai rencontrée', *Flûte à bec et instruments anciens* XV (1985), pp4-5

is now discredited, but the first formative description of the instrument, its compass and technique come from Mersenne's *Harmonie Universelle* of 1636. The instrument is described as being some 12 cm in length, with four finger-holes in the front and two thumb-holes behind and with a recorder-like beak. The compass of the instrument was two octaves (d''' to d''''') and its music was transposed down two octaves. Around the middle of the seventeenth century the flageolet arrived in England and gained considerable popularity as an amateur's instrument until its decline after the first third of the eighteenth century: it attracted few professional players, but it has been suggested that the *flautino* parts in Handel's *Rinaldo* and *Acis and Galatea* were written for the flageolet. The use of the instrument as a 'bird flageolet' for teaching birds to sing dates from the early part of the eighteenth century, and it is at this time that the sponge chamber made its first appearance (see below). The English flageolet dating from the late eighteenth or early nineteenth century is a very different instrument, and bears considerably more resemblance to the recorder than does the traditional French flageolet.

The English flageolet was never standardized: it had six or seven finger holes, sometimes a thumb-hole, and from one to six keys with a compass of two octaves from d''. Ivory studs were often fitted to the instrument in order to guide the player's fingers to the tone-holes, and, on some instruments, the names of the notes were inscribed upon the instrument. The flageolet usually had a fine mouthpiece of bone or ivory which led to a chamber containing a sponge to absorb moisture from the player's breath. The English maker William Bainbridge (fl1803-1834) made several developments to the simple flageolet, including the 'flute flageolet' (which was played transversely) and the complex double and triple flageolets. The double flageolet consisted of two flageolets set side-by-side and fed from a common sponge chamber so that (by means of a complex fingering system, aided by keys) the player could play on one or both pipes, the latter technique permitting simple harmonization in thirds and sixths. The uncommon triple flageolet had a third pipe with four keys, and worked on the same principle as the ocarina. Many of these instruments survive, but they were essentially amateur's instruments although there is small repertoire for the flageolet as an obbligato instrument with singer and keyboard; production of English flageolets diminished as the nineteenth century drew to its close.

In France, the traditional flageolet with four finger- and two thumb-holes continued in use throughout the nineteenth century in salon and dance bands and was occasionally employed in military bands as a piccolo substitute: it bore the name *quadrille flageolet*. The instrument was usually built in the key of A and had a shrill, penetrating tone, usually possessed a sponge chamber and acquired more keywork as the century progressed, leading eventually to the Boehm model with multiple keys and rings. Unlike the English flageolet, the French instrument was played by several virtuosi including Collinet and Bousquet, some of whose music is now available in transposition for the recorder.

*Introduction*

The English flageolet (as well as the French) was also played in Germany and a Wiener Flageolet (of similar design to the English instrument) achieved a certain popularity in Vienna during the nineteenth century. For further information on the csakan and flageolet, the reader is referred to publications by Betz, Meierott and Moeck (see bibliography).

The above comments serve to outline a brief history of the two most significant duct flutes of the nineteenth century: many other types of duct flute existed throughout – and beyond – Europe in this period, but it is not within the scope of the present work to discuss these instruments, whose details varied from country to country. Walking-stick (cane) recorders and double recorders are likewise excluded from the study. Many compositions from the csakan and flageolet repertoire are currently in print, arranged for the recorder: it has to be admitted that many of these pieces are of poor quality and lacking in musical interest, but nevertheless allow the recorder player to explore a duct flute repertoire dating from the days when the recorder was largely unseen and unheard – but, as Rachel Barnes eloquently summarised the situation in her thesis on the recorder from 1740-1900 – 'The Recorder – obsolete and eclipsed?'

Before studying the history of the recorder in the nineteenth century, it is appropriate to examine the reasons for its decline as the eighteenth century drew to its close.

*The Recorder In The Nineteenth Century*

# CHAPTER II

## THE DECLINE OF THE RECORDER IN THE EIGHTEENTH CENTURY

During the latter half of the eighteenth century, the recorder declined in popularity, with fewer recorders being made and few pieces of music specifically being written for the instrument. Curiously, many of these later pieces called for the use of small recorders as obbligato instruments in vocal music (particularly by English composers such as Arne and Shield) but the last documented use of the instrument in opera was as an accompaniment (for alto recorder) to the aria *Rien ne me peut calmer ma peine* in Giovanni Paisiello's *Barber of Seville* of 1782. In parallel with the decline in popularity of the instrument, fewer treatises ('self- tutors') were published.

By 1784 the German author and composer C. F. D. Schubart was to write of *Die Flaute doulce*:

*Der allzu leise Ton, und der geringe Umfang des Instruments, hat es heut zu tage beynahe aus der mode gebracht: man hört es weder in der Kirche , noch bey Concerten [sic] mehr.* (on account of its quiet tone and the small compass the instrument is not today in fashion: it is no longer heard in the church or in concerts.)[4]

These few words in German perhaps sum up the principal reasons for the decline of the recorder, but further consideration needs to be given to examine the topic in detail and to reflect on the comments of notable authors of the period. Those giants amongst eighteenth century musical historians Dr Charles Burney (1726-1814) and Sir John Hawkins (1719-1789) both made interesting references to the recorder in the 1770s. During his travels in Italy, Burney heard a recorder player in Florence in 1770:

After dinner, went to a great accademia at Mr. Hampson's, an old English Gent. where I heard Nardini... little Linley, the master of the house who plays the Common Flute (i.e. recorder – author) in a peculiar manner, blowing it through a spunge.[5]

The instrument was most probably a flageolet, but capped recorders (the cap containing a sponge) are not entirely unknown. It is reasonable to expect a musician of Dr. Burney's erudition to know the difference between a flageolet and a recorder, but not all flageolets had sponge-caps at this period and the term 'Common Flute' certainly implied recorder.

---

4   Schubart, C.F.D. , *Ideen zur einer Aesthetik der Tonkunst*, (Hildesheim: Georg Oluns modern edition 1990), p322
5   Burney, C., *Men, Music and Manners in France and Italy*, (London: Eulenberg [for the Folio Society] modern edition 1969), p116

## The Recorder In The Nineteenth Century

Hawkins noted that the recorder ('flute' in his terminology) was a popular instrument amongst gentlemen in the early eighteenth century, the fashion for its use coming from France, and he illustrates a bewigged gentleman playing a recorder from a book of instructions which was published around 1700. Hawkins continues:

> And to come nearer to our own time [1786], it may be remembered by many now living, that a flute was the pocket companion of many who wished to be thought fine gentlemen.

But he goes on to say:

> ...the practice of the flûte à bec descended to the young apprentices of tradesmen, and was the amusement of their winter evenings.[6]

Hawkins (who displayed a somewhat caustic attitude to wind players) here infers that the recorder is passing out of the realm of serious art music.

In 1801 Thomas Busby published his *Complete Dictionary of Music*, a search through its pages yielding three entries of relevance, these pointing again to the gradual obsolescence of the recorder:[7]

### RECORDER

An old wind instrument somewhat resembling a flute; but of a smaller bore and of a shriller tone. It is said to have six holes, and to have answered to the tibia minor, or flajeolet [sic] of Mersenne. This instrument has been by some musical authors confounded with the flute; and we meet with old books of instruction for the flute, the directions of which are also professedly given for the recorder.

### FLUTE A BEC

See flute, common

---

[6] Hawkins, J., *A General history of the Science and Practice of Music*, (New York: Dover Publications Inc. modern edition 1963), pp338-9
[7] Busby, T.A., *A Complete Dictionary of Music. To which is prefixed a familiar Introduction to the First Principles of that Science*, (London: R Phillips 1801)

**FLUTE, COMMON**

A wind instrument consisting of a tube about 18" in length with eight holes. Formerly called 'Flûte à bec' from the old Gaulish word 'Bec' signifying the beak of a cockerel. Now indifferently called the Common Flute or English Flute to distinguish it from the German Flute.

The degree of uncertainty displayed in these descriptions suggest that Busby was not overtly familiar with the recorder, probably because it was not in common use at the time he compiled his dictionary. His description of 'recorder' could fit with the French flageolet of Mersenne which possessed six holes (4+2), and it should be recalled that, in early eighteenth century England, the recorder was simply called 'flute', subsequently acquiring the names 'common flute' and English flute'.

On the other side of the English Channel the encyclopédiste Framèry regretted the passing of the recorder in his *Encyclopédie méthodique* of 1791 but a recorder is illustrated in the great *Encyclopédie* of Diderot et d'Alembert which was published between 1751 and 1765. The comments of Schubart (quoted above) suffice to underline a similar perception of the decline of the recorder in Germany.

Well into the days of the recorder's revival, Macauley Fitzgibbon, writing in 1934, made an interesting observation:

> it [the recorder] began to die out in France about 1750 but it survived in Germany to a later date and is said to have been played in a concert in England in 1800.[8]

Unfortunately he gives no source for his tantalizing comment about the use of a recorder in a concert in England in 1800. Current evidence (in the form of extant recorders) does not entirely substantiate his claim about the recorder dying out in France as early as 1750 and it is now known that the instrument survived in parts of southern Germany well into the latter part of the nineteenth century.

The perception in the literature is that the recorder virtually ceased to exist after the middle of the eighteenth century. However, it is seldom that any artefact of mankind passes suddenly into oblivion: the process of extinction is more often one of a period of obsolescence preceding obscurity, the lute, for example, (whose heyday was in the sixteenth and early seventeenth centuries) lingering on in occasional use long enough for J. S. Bach to have composed for it. In 1957 Dolmetsch summarised the situation with regard to the recorder:

---

[8] Macauley Fitzgibbon, H., 'Of Flutes and soft Recorders', *Musical Quarterly* XX /2 (1934), pp219-229

The recorder is supposed to have become obsolescent during the 1760s. I am inclined to think that the process was more gradual and that it lingered on here and there until it and the 'German flute' [i.e., the transverse baroque flute] were definitely superseded by Boehm's 'modern' flute.[9]

In my paper in *The Consort* of 1983, I noted that recorders continued to be made well into the nineteenth century and that both music and treatises for the instrument continued to appear (admittedly in rapidly decreasing quantity) until the last years of the eighteenth century.[10] Before studying the history of the recorder in the nineteenth century it is pertinent to examine the causes of its decline in the eighteenth: two strands of discussion become apparent, the first relating to changes in musical culture in the eighteenth century, the second to the nature of the instrument itself in relation to these changes.

## CHANGES IN MUSICAL CULTURE IN THE EIGHTEENTH CENTURY

At the beginning of the eighteenth century, Europe gloried in the splendour of the high baroque: by the end of the century, revolution and romanticism pervaded European culture. Substantial philosophical, sociological, theological – and consequently aesthetic – changes occurred and it is during the course of these changes that the recorder passed from being a commonplace instrument to one of obscurity.

The underlying philosophical changes were those of the Enlightenment, a movement led by such philosophers as Voltaire and Rousseau, authors such as Goethe and Schiller, a movement which placed reason and experience above superstition and inherited prejudice. The philosophy of the Enlightenment led to the overturning of many traditional structures (exemplified by the French Revolution, which became apparent with the storming of the Bastille in 1789), the rise of the bourgeoisie and middle classes, and a scourging of much aristocratic privilege. The aesthetic principles of the Enlightenment (led by the philosopher, critic and composer Jean-Jacques Rousseau, 1712-1778) placed an emphasis on nature and feeling over and against the rigid conventions of the baroque era, and, in a sense, preparing the way for the romantic movement of the early nineteenth century. Musically, the statuesque grandeur of Bach had given way to the emotional turbulence of Beethoven, passing on its journey through the classical era of Haydn and Mozart.

Baroque music – the music of the zenith of the recorder's popularity – is characterized by a non-dramatic formal style in which the long-term use of key change (essentially between movements) involves little tonal conflict within each individual movement

---

9 Dolmetsch, C.F., 'The Recorder and Flute in the eighteenth Century', *The Consort* XIV (1957), pp18-23
10 MacMillan, D., 'The Recorder in the late eighteenth and early nineteenth Centuries', *The Consort* XXXIX (1983), p489-497

although there may well be episodes of rhythmic conflict such as syncopation: each movement expresses its own emotions. Movements written before 1750 tended to be based on a single idea and governed by a single *Affekt*, contrast only occurring between opposing planes (such as loud/soft) whereas movements written after 1750 tend to contain contrast within themselves.[11] Formal conventions (for example, the *da capo* aria) abounded in the late baroque era, the use of instrumental obbligato accompaniment was common (of considerable relevance to the recorder repertoire), and the entire harmonic structure was supported by a *basso continuo* played on an organ, harpsichord or theorbo with 'cello, bass viol or bassoon playing the bass line. The term *style galant* described this type of music – music which was modern, current and in fashion, appealing to the widest audience because of its innate simplicity over and against the complex polyphonic and contrapunctal styles of previous generations.

As the eighteenth century progressed the unchallenging *style galant* of the late baroque gave way to the *Empfindsamer Stil*, a movement originating in north Germany and whose principal exponent was C.P.E.Bach. *Empfindsamkeit* represents a style of sensitivity and sensibility (using the latter word in its derivative sense), a showing of an increased emotional and expressive trend in music but in the 1770s the *Sturm und Drang* (storm and stress) style emerged, portraying yet more violent emotion in musical composition. The progression from the *style galant* towards romanticism was becoming increasingly apparent: the age of Enlightenment may well have been the age of reason but the arts were beginning to break free from the constricts of pure reason to portray the depths of human emotional experience, the encyclopédiste d'Alembert commenting that 'music not only aims to please, but also to excite the emotions'. Elegant simplicity was giving way to emotional turbulence, the *Sturm and Drang* movement being sometimes described as 'proto-romanticism'.

During the latter part of the eighteenth century, sonata form (described by Mellers as 'more a principle than a form') came into being and became the foundation upon which the classical sonatas, concertos and symphonies of Haydn, Mozart, Beethoven and many lesser masters were built. It became the dominant form in the field of instrumental music and may be contrasted directly with baroque formality in that tonal development and contrast occur *within* the movement itself, leading to a deeper sense of emotional conflict. The baroque concept of contrast essentially *between* movements had been superseded by emotional contrast *within* the movement.

In parallel with the development of sonata form, the keyboard sonata, the string quartet and the symphony expanded in length and complexity. The development of the symphony is of particular relevance to the study of the decline of the recorder, for classical symphonies increasingly called for larger and more powerful orchestras, typified by the

---

11  *New Grove Dictionary of Music and Musicians ('New Grove II')*, (London: Macmillan 2nd edition 2001), s.v. 'Sonata Form' (Webster, J.)

famous Mannheim orchestra. The instruments themselves were becoming louder (the Tourte bow was developed in the mid-eighteenth century) and dynamic contrasts became greater. The recorder's cousin and rival the transverse flute began to acquire more keys to improve its range and intonation and the previously conical foot-joint became cylindrical in order to enhance the power of the lower register, a process which was to culminate in the fully-keyed and fully-cylindrical Boehm flute of the mid-nineteenth century. The basso continuo and elaborate counterpoint had largely been replaced by an homophonic texture with oboes and horns supporting the harmony: lengthy obbligato passages for wind instruments were seldom written. Musical practice seldom undergoes sudden global change and older (and often lesser) composers continued to write in the older style while the more forward-thinking men introduced changes, yet inevitably only the more wealthy organizations could afford to employ large orchestras. Sociologically, there was a shift from the small court concert room or theatre to larger concert halls and opera houses, for the Enlightenment had paved the way for a new 'middle class' with sufficient money and leisure to enjoy what were hitherto aristocratic privileges – art, theatre and music.

As the consort music of the renaissance gave way to the sonatas, suites and concerto of the baroque, the recorder developed both in timbre and compass: as the baroque gave way to the emotionally more expressive and musically larger forces of the classical and early romantic periods, the gentle recorder – with its limited dynamic range and limited potential for development – found itself displaced by the ever-evolving transverse flute.

## THE RECORDER EXAMINED

Peter, writing in 1953, gives the classic explanation for the decline of the recorder:

> After the middle of the eighteenth century hardly any music makes a serious use of the recorder. The age in which an instrument like the recorder had its friends and lovers had now passed. There was a general striving after a greater volume of sound with its appeal to man's emotions rather than to the timeless being that reigns over him. Recorders were superseded by flutes, viols by violins, harpsichords by pianos. So the instrument fell into almost complete oblivion for more than 150 years.[12]

MacGillivray concurs with this view, writing:

> The main reason why it was superseded was the increased preoccupation with nuance and dynamic range. With its fixed sound-generator the recorder belonged

---

[12] Peter, H., *The Recorder, its Tradition and Tasks*, trans. Godman, S., (London: Hinrichsen Edition Ltd. 1953), p59

## The decline of the Recorder in the Eighteenth Century

to a vanishing world of simple formal phrasing and level organ-like dynamics.[13]

In 1967 the American recorder player Daniel Waitzman challenged this seemingly cogent explanation – based as it is on the relationship between the changes in music and the relative immutability of the recorder – with six propositions which are worthy of examination:[14]

1. The recorder lacked a significant class of professional players.

There were many amateur players but Waitzman suggests (no doubt correctly) that most professional recorder playing was accomplished by men who were players of other instruments.* He notes the technical difficulty of some eighteenth-century recorder music (such as Bach's Brandenburg Concerti and the concerti of Telemann) but observes that most recorder music was not of great difficulty and could be played by amateurs who often studied from treatises which themselves reached only a moderate level of technical ability. He comments upon the greater flexibility of the flute and oboe and suggests that recorder players of the period could have acquired a better *messa di voce* had they been so inclined. I believe that these comments are entirely reasonable.

2. The recorder's true nature was not generally appreciated, even at the height of its popularity.

Waitzman believes that most composers saw the recorder as a gentle and 'pastoral' instrument, rather than considering it a more passionate one when its higher register is exploited: he, however, sees the recorder as a 'clarino flute'. On close examination of the repertoire, however, one finds relatively few pieces which use the instrument in a 'clarino' role and I consider that the composers of the baroque would have used the recorder (as they would have used any other instrument) when its individual timbre was appropriate. To assert that a common instrument was not appreciated tends to belittle the composers who wrote for it, with the lower and middle registers of the alto recorder frequently (and successfully) employed in pieces where a pastoral, other-worldly or mournful effect was desired. The high register of the alto is indeed brilliant, but Waitzman fails to consider the equally brilliant sound of the fifth and sixth flutes, a brilliance which is present throughout the compass of these small recorders. His remarks appear to be confined entirely to the alto recorder, and he ignores the brilliant concerti for small recorders by the English

---

13    MacGillivray, J.A., in *Musical Instruments throughout the Ages*, ed. Baines, A., (London: Penguin 1961), p243
14    Waitzman, D., 'The Decline of the Recorder in the eighteenth Century', *The American Recorder* VIII/2 (1967), pp47-51
\* it is not uncommon to find in orchestral works calling for both oboes and recorders that the two instruments do not play simultaneously, suggesting that the players 'doubled'.

composers of the early eighteenth century.

3. The high tessitura of the soloistic alto recorder discouraged composers from writing idiomatically for the instrument.
   The more likely explanation is that composers did not write such music as few would have been able to play it and few copies would have been sold.

4. The exploitation of the highest registers of the recorder posed special problems for eighteenth-century recorder makers and players.
   Waitzman indicates that the highest notes of the recorder (i.e. in the third octave) are either 'impossible, out-of-tune or ugly' unless the bell can be temporarily closed. He suggests that, had the bell-key (invented by Carl Dolmetsch in 1929) been available, the recorder might have been able 'to hold its own throughout the eighteenth century'. This argument is speculative.

5. With the rise of the post-baroque style, there was a lessening interest in clarino instruments.
   The clarino style of trumpet playing was essentially a baroque phenomenon.

6. All these factors interacted with one another, giving the recorder bad reputation and discouraging serious students from studying the instrument.

Throughout these propositions Waitzman concentrates on the highest registers of the alto recorder, one of the more technically demanding aspects of both making and playing the instrument. As indicated above, few baroque works call for the continued (as opposed to occasional) use of the higher reaches of the second octave, and most recorder music lies within the lower and middle registers (a range of a little over one and a half octaves) – well within the ability of the good amateur. Composers employed recorders to express the specific *Affekt* which its unique timbre engenders, this often being reflective in style (e.g. Bach's use of the recorder in his *Actus Tragicus* [Cantata 106]): composers would also have an eye on their livelihood, and would be more likely to publish works which were within the ability of the large corpus of amateur players, rather than writing for the eclectic few professionals. It is surprising that Waitzman gives no consideration to the (admittedly small) repertoire for the fifth and sixth flutes.

Waitzman describes the decline of the recorder in terms of *his* perception of the instrument rather than in terms of the cultural changes which precipitated its gradual obsolescence. That the recorder was not modified is beyond question: whether such development was technically possible at the time is open to debate. Music had changed, but the recorder had not (or could not) change with it.

*The decline of the Recorder in the Eighteenth Century*

Dolmetsch, in 1957, took a different view:

It has been stated more than once that, in the eighteenth century, the transverse flute usurped the place of the recorder. This is totally untrue. Having supplied the needs of all kinds of music-making, be they sociable consorts or simple tunes and dances, the recorder kept pace with the tremendous developments in chamber music, solos, and concertos in the eighteenth century, and, rising to the occasion, proved that it could serve the virtuoso as well.[15]

Unfortunately there is little evidence to support this statement. Were it true, the recorder would not have passed into relative obscurity for almost a century.

## CONCLUSION

It is an established historical fact that the recorder declined in use after the middle of the eighteenth century: fewer instruments were made, less music specified its use, and the number of published treatises progressively diminished. During this period of history, music underwent cataclysmic changes from the formality of the baroque to the unbridled emotion of the early romantic era, a movement rooted in the philosophical and cultural *milieu* of the Enlightenment, with the arts increasingly expressing the depths of human emotion. Individual instruments became more flexible in dynamic range and louder in sonority: ensembles grew from small court bands to substantial symphony orchestras.

Of the authors who discuss the decline of the recorder, Peter relates the phenomenon to changes in musical culture. Waitzman argues that the true nature of the recorder was not understood by composers, basing his observations on the higher range of the alto recorder and ignoring the traditional uses to which the instrument was put and also underestimating the significance of the amateur. He does not appear to relate the diminishing popularity of the recorder to the changes in musical culture but prefers to blame both the lack of development of the instrument and the composers' lack of understanding of the instrument's nature. Dolmetsch's argument that the recorder continued to keep pace with the developments in music is hardly credible to the historian.

I believe that the recorder declined in popularity during the latter years of the eighteenth century as it was no longer suited to the musical style of the period. That it declined in use is certain: that it did not become extinct is equally certain – as subsequent pages of this small book will demonstrate.

---

15   Dolmetsch, C.F., 'The Recorder and Flute in the eighteenth Century'

*The Recorder In The Nineteenth Century*

# CHAPTER III

## INVENTORY OF RECORDERS

### 1800 – 1905

The prime evidence for the use of a musical instrument in any period of history is the continued (or reinstated) manufacture of that instrument, and a search for recorders built between 1800 and 1905 yielded a total of 115 instruments: in sixty-eight cases the name of the maker is identified. A further group of nine recorders built at the turn of the eighteenth and nineteenth centuries is added to this number. These may be of late eighteenth-or early nineteenth-century origin although their precise date of manufacture cannot be discerned, but the recorders are of interest as they demonstrate a continuing tradition of recorder making up to the beginning of the nineteenth century. Finally, an heterogenous group of twenty-three instruments is added, bringing the total to 147. The present location of some of these is not known, some are of hybrid type, some may be of early twentieth century origin, and others are presented for discussion as being of organological interest. Some are presented to correct misunderstandings in the literature, or to demonstrate attempts to develop and improve the basic baroque recorder. For ease of reference, each instrument has been allocated a 'MacMillan Number' which will be used throughout the book. The inventory has been compiled from a study of organological reference books (notably Waterhouse's *The New Langwill Index* and Young's *4900 Historical Woodwind Instruments*), together with museum catalogues and journals in order to obtain as much detail as may be discerned about the instruments: visits were made to collections both in the United Kingdom and overseas and internet sites examined. Of these, Lander's Recorder Home Page and its database of recorders was of particular importance. Personal communication was established (electronically, by mail, and by telephone) with scholars, many of whom provided extracts from museum catalogues containing details of recorders. I gratefully acknowledge the help of these men and women who gave their time to replying to my many queries. The major sources of reference are listed in the bibliography.

### PLAN OF THE INVENTORY

The most significant instruments are those whose makers can be identified by name and so can be dated with some accuracy with regard to the years between which they were made. Sixty-eight such instruments have been identified and are given the prefix 'N'. Some of these recorders form part of a continued tradition of recorder-making, whilst others are products of the recorder revival. Secondly, forty-seven recorders whose makers cannot be identified (most often because they bear no stamp) are listed under the prefix 'A'. The evidence for a nineteenth-century origin of many of these lies in the expertise of the curators of the museums in which they are located, but cross-referencing within the present study has substantially confirmed the nineteenth century origin of some of this group of recorders (notably A2, A7, A8, A34, and A35 compared with N5 and N45) and A24 compared with the Berchtesgaden recorders (N57 - N68). Nine recorders made at the turn of the eighteenth and nineteenth centuries are prefixed 'E' and the twenty-three heterogenous instruments (about which there is uncertainty or debate) are prefixed 'D'.

Information regarding the maker, location, and type of each instrument is given (where known): as much detail as may be discerned regarding length, materials, keywork, maker's mark, and provenance is listed. Biographical information is given only for the first recorder by any given maker, the second (and subsequent) instruments only bearing the maker's name. The source(s) for the information is/are given (often several for each recorder), and, where appropriate, the instrument is discussed. The pitch of the lowest note (where known) is given: this can only be approximate for the pitch standard (in cycles per second) is seldom specified. Details of bore dimensions, and the size and position of tone-holes, are beyond the scope of the present work.

Three recorders no longer extant are included for completeness: the makers of these instruments is known, but the recorders themselves were lost in the Second World War.

It is improbable that this inventory of recorders built between 1800 and 1905 is complete, for other instruments will almost certainly exist in small museums and inaccessible private collections. However, the list as it stands provides, at least, an overview of recorder making between the years of 1800 and 1905.

### INDEX OF THE INVENTORY

#### 'N' SERIES RECORDERS

| | | |
|---|---|---|
| N1 | Bellissent | F – Paris : Musée de la Musique |
| N2 | Billing | D - Halle: Händelhaus |
| N3 | Camus | CH – Basel : Historisches Museum |
| N4 | Camus | F – Paris : Musée de la Musique |
| N5 | Colas | USA – MI – Ann Arbor: Stearns Collection |
| N6 | Dupré | B – Brussels : Musée des Instruments de Musique |

*Inventory of Recorders*

| | | |
|---|---|---|
| N7 | Galpin | US – MA – Boston: Museum of Fine arts |
| N8 | Galpin | US – MA – Boston: Museum of Fine Arts |
| N9 | Galpin | US – MA – Boston: Museum of Fine Arts |
| N10 | Galpin | US – MA – Boston: Museum of Fine Arts |
| N11 | Garsi | I – Parma: Conservatorio |
| N12 | Gerlach | D – Bavaria: anonymous private collection |
| N13 | Goulding | US – PA – Philadelphia: Oster (dealer) |
| N14 | Goulding | J – Tokyo: Iino (private collection) |
| N15 | Goulding | GB – London: Victoria and Albert Museum |
| N16 | Goulding | US – NY – New York: Metropolitan Museum of Art |
| N17 | Goulding | D – Celle: Moeck (private collection) |
| N18 | Gras | F – Paris: Musée de la Musique |
| N19 | Hochschwarzer | D – Sigmaringen: Schloss |
| N20 | Jeantet | F – Paris: Musée de la Musique |
| N21 | Kruspe | US – MI – Ann Arbor: Stearns Collection |
| N22 | Lamy | F – Paris: Musée de la Musique |
| N23 | Lecomte | F – Paris: Sallaberry (private collection) |
| N24 | Lecomte | F – Paris: Sallaberry (private collection) |
| N25 | Löhner FII | CH – Basel : Historisches Museum |
| N26 | Löhner F II | CH – Basel: Historisches Museum |

| | | |
|---|---|---|
| N27 | Löhner J A | D – Erlangen : Universität |
| N28 | Löhner J A | S – Stockholm : Musikmuseet |
| N29 | Mahillon | I – Florence : Conservatorio |
| N30 | Mahillon | I – Florence : Conservatorio |
| N31 | Mahillon | B – Brussels : Musée des Instruments de Musique |
| N32 | Mahillon | B – Brussels : Musée des Instruments de Musique |
| N33 | Mahillon | B – Brussels : Musée des Instruments de Musique |
| N34 | Mahillon | B – Brussels : Musée des Instruments de Musique |
| N35 | Mahillon | B – Brussels : Musée des Instruments de Musique |
| N36 | Mahillon | B – Brussels : Musée des Instruments de Musique |
| N37 | Mahillon | B – Brussels : Musée des Instruments de Musique |
| N38 | Mahillon | B – Brussels : Musée des Instruments de Musique |
| N39 | Mahillon | B – Brussels : Musée des Instruments de Musique |
| N40 | Mahillon | B – Brussels : Musée des Instruments de Musique |
| N41 | Mahillon | B – Brussels : Musée des Instruments de Musique |
| N42 | Mahillon | B – Brussels : Musée des Instruments de Musique |
| N43 | Martin J-B | F – Paris: Musée de la Musique |
| N44 | Martin J G | D – Leipzig: Universität |
| N45 | Noblet | GB- Oxford: Bate Collection |
| N46 | Noblet & Thibouville | D – Berlin: Institut für Musikforschung (x) |

| | | |
|---|---|---|
| N47 | Noblet & Thibouville | D – Berlin: Institut für Musikforschung (x) |
| N48 | Noblet & Thibouville | D – Celle : Moeck (private collection) |
| N49 | Oppenheim | GB – Oxford: Bate Collection |
| N50 | Schin | D – Nuremberg: Germanisches Nationalmuseum |
| N51 | Schweffer | A – Graz: Landesmuseum Johanneum |
| N52 | Schweffer | A – Graz: Landesmuseum Johanneum |
| N53 | Thibouville-Cabart | D – Leipzig : Universität |
| N54 | Thibouville-Cabart | I – Milan: Museo Castello Sforzesco |
| N55 | Tolbecque | F – Paris : Musée de la Musique |
| N56 | Townsend | Unknown |
| N57 | Walch L II | D – Munich: Deutsches Museum |
| N58 | Walch L II | A – Salzburg: Museo Carolino Augusteum |
| N59 | Walch L II | US – DC – Washington: DCM |
| N60 | Walch L II | D – Bonn: Beethovenhaus |
| N61 | Walch L II | D – Berchtesgaden: Heimatmuseum |
| N62 | Walch L II | D – Berchtesgaden: Heimatmuseum |
| N63 | Walch L II | D – Stuttgart: Hase (private collection) |
| N64 | Walch L II | D – Nuremberg: Germanisches Nationalmuseum |
| N65 | Walch P | A – Salzburg: Museo Carolino Augusteum |
| N66 | Walch P | D – Nuremberg: Germanisches Nationalmuseum |

| | | |
|---|---|---|
| N67 | Walch P | D – Nuremberg: Germanisches Nationalmuseum |
| N68 | Walch P | D – Bremen: Müller (private collection) |

## 'A' SERIES RECORDERS

| | | |
|---|---|---|
| A1 | Unknown | F – Paris: Musée de la Musique |
| A2 | Unknown | F – Paris: Musée de la Musique |
| A3 | Unknown | F – Paris: Musée de la Musique |
| A4 | Unknown | F – Paris: Musée de la Musique |
| A5 | Unknown | F – Paris: Musée de la Musique |
| A6 | Unknown | F – Paris: Musée de la Musique |
| A7 | Unknown | F – Paris: Musée de la Musique |
| A8 | Unknown | F – Paris: Musée de la Musique |
| A9 | Unknown | F – Paris: Musée de la Musique |
| A10 | Unknown | F – Paris: Musée de la Musique |
| A11 | Unknown | F – Paris: Musée de la Musique |
| A12 | Unknown | F – Paris: Musée de la Musique |
| A13 | Unknown | F – La Couture-Boussey: Musée |
| A14 | Unknown | F – La Couture-Boussey: Musée |
| A15 | Unknown | F – La Couture-Boussey: Musée |
| A16 | Unknown | F – La Couture-Boussey: Musée |

*Inventory of Recorders*

| | | |
|---|---|---|
| A17 | Unknown | F – La Couture-Boussey: Musée |
| A18 | Unknown | F – La Couture-Boussey: Musée |
| A19 | Unknown | F – La Couture-Boussey: Musée |
| A20 | Unknown | F – La Couture-Boussey: Musée |
| A21 | Unknown | F – Marseille: Musée Grobet-Labadié |
| A22 | Unknown | F – Marseille: Musée Grobet-Labadié |
| A23 | Unknown | F – Nice: Musée Masséna |
| A24 | Unknown | DK – Copenhagen: Musikhistorisk Museum |
| A25 | Unknown | DK – Copenhagen: Musikhistorisk Museum |
| A26 | Unknown | DK – Copenhagen: Musikhistorisk Museum |
| A27 | Unknown | DK – Copenhagen: Musikhistorisk museum |
| A28 | Unknown | NL - The Hague: Gemeentemuseum |
| A29 | Unknown | NL – The Hague: Gemeentemuseum |
| A30 | Unknown | NL – The Hague: Gemeentemuseum |
| A31 | Unknown | D – Nuremberg: Germanisches Nationalmuseum |
| A32 | Unknown | A – Graz – S: Stadtmuseum |
| A33 | Unknown | GB – London: Horniman Museum |
| A34 | Unknown | B – Brussels: Musée des Instruments de Musique |
| A35 | Unknown | US – MI – Ann Arbor: Stearns Collection |
| A36 | Unknown | US – NY – New York : Metropolitan Museum of Art |

| | | |
|---|---|---|
| A37 | Unknown | US – NY – New York : Metropolitan Museum of Art |
| A38 | Unknown | US – NY – New York : Metropolitan Museum of Art |
| A39 | Unknown | US – NY – New York: Metropolitan Museum of Art |
| A40 | Unknown | US – NY – New York : Metropolitan Museum of Art |
| A41 | Unknown | US – NY – New York : Metropolitan Museum of Art |
| A42 | Unknown | US - NY – New York:  Metropolitan Museum of Art |
| A43 | Unknown | US – NY – New York : Metropolitan Museum of Art |
| A44 | Unknown | US – NY – New York : Metropolitan Museum of Art |
| A45 | Unknown | US – DC – Washington: Smithsonian |
| A46 | Unknown | ?US – CA - Claremont: Fiske |
| A47 | Unknown | Australia-Sydney: Powerhouse Museum |

## E SERIES RECORDERS

| | | |
|---|---|---|
| E 1 | Grassi | I – Rome: Museo degli Strumenti Musicale |
| E 2 | Grassi | D – Leipzig : Universität |
| E 3 | Grenser | D – Berlin : Institut für Musikforschung (x) |
| E 4 | Walch L I | A – Salzburg: Museo Carolino Augusteum |
| E 5 | Walch L I | D – Bavaria: secret private collection |
| E 6 | Walch L I | D – Berchtesgaden: Heimatmuseum |
| E 7 | Walch L I | D – Berchtesgaden: Heimatmuseum |

| E 8  | Anon | US – DC – Washington: DCM |
|------|------|---------------------------|
| E 9  | Anon | CH – Reinach: Tarasov (private collection) |

## D SERIES RECORDERS

| D1  | Bainbridge | Unknown |
|-----|------------|---------|
| D2  | ?Bertani | I – Modena : Museo Civico d'Arte |
| D3  | Boie | N – Trondheim : Ringve Museum |
| D4  | Destuyver | B – Brussels : Musée des Instruments de Musique |
| D5  | Firth, Pond, & Co. | Unknown |
| D6  | ?Galpin | US – MA – Boston: Museum of Fine Arts |
| D7  | Goulding, D'Almaine | Unknown |
| D8  | Lot | Unknown |
| D9  | ?Martin | F – La Couture-Boussey : Musée |
| D10 | Rudall, Carte, & Co. | GB – Oxford: Bate Collection |
| D11 | Sattler (family) | D – Leipzig: Universität |
| D12 | Smart | US – DC – Washington: DCM |
| D13 | Wrede | US – NC – Duke: Eddy Collection, Duke University |
| D14 | Unknown ?Hotteterre | GB – London: Royal College of Music |
| D15 | Unknown ?Metzler | Unknown |
| D16 | Unknown | US – DC – Washington: Smithsonian |
| D17 | Unknown | GB – Oxford: Bate Collection |

| D18 | French | US – MA – Boston: Museum of Fine Arts |
| D19 | Unknown | US – DC – Washington: DCM |
| D20 | Unknown | US – DC – Washington: Museum of Fine Arts |
| D21 | AE | NL – The Hague: Gemeentemuseum |
| D22 | ?Tolbecque | US – DC – Washington: DCM |
| D23 | Hawkes | GB – Stockport: Turner (private collection) |

## THE RECORDERS

### N 1

| | |
|---|---|
| MAKER | BELLISSENT |
| DATES | fl a1819 – 1842 |
| PLACE OF WORK | Paris (F) |
| LOCATION | F – Paris: Musée de la Musique |
| COLLECTION NUMBER | E 2137 |
| TYPE | Tenor |
| LOWEST NOTE | a (ancien diapason) |
| LENGTH | 557 mm |
| MATERIALS/MOUNTS | Ebony: ivory mounts: clarinet-like bell: 4 pieces |
| KEYS | 7: nickel silver |
| MARK | (lyre)/ BELLISSENT/ A PARIS/ (crowned#) |
| PROVENANCE | ex Cesbron (157), donated to museum 1934 |
| SOURCES | Collection on-line catalogue: Lander: museum visit |

This instrument comes from the collection of Paul Cesbron dated 1906. It has a clarinet-like bell and seven keys, the lowest of which extends the downward range of the recorder. The pitch *ancien diapason* refers to the pitch prevailing at the time of manufacture: in 1858 (somewhat later than the date the recorder was made) *diapason normal* in France stood at a' 435 cps whereas the remainder of Europe placed a' at 446. The recorder is therefore at a low pitch. The keywork bears no similarity to that of a similarly-dated French recorder by Jeantet (N 20).

Bellissent was listed as a maker of flutes in 1819, and the following year as a music dealer. In 1830 he was described as a supplier of flutes. He made a number of improvements to the (transverse) flute but no other recorders of his manufacture appear to be extant: a flute, a piccolo, and a fife survive (*New Langwill*).

## N 2

| | |
|---|---|
| MAKER | BILLING, Friedrich |
| DATES | b c1777   d1825   fl 1808 – 1825 |
| PLACE OF WORK | Warsaw (PL) |
| LOCATION | D – Halle: Handelhaus |
| TYPE | Sopranino |
| MARK | (lily)/ F.BILLING/ A.VARSOVIE/ (flower) |
| SOURCE | *New Langwill* |

No other details are known: a clarinet exists.

## N 3

| | |
|---|---|
| MAKER | CAMUS |
| DATES | fl 1793 – 1822 |
| PLACE OF WORK | Paris (F) |
| LOCATION | CH – Basel: Historisches Museum |
| COLLECTION NUMBER | 1994.267 |
| TYPE | Voice Flute |
| LOWEST NOTE | d' |
| MARK | (lion looking to left with raised paws)/ CAMUS/ A PARIS/ (sun). The stamps on the lower two joints omit 'A PARIS' |
| SOURCES | Gutmann (personal communication 2002): Lander: museum visit |

Gutmann considers that this recorder may be by the noted French flautist Paul Hippolyte Camus (b Paris 1796). The mark, however, is consistent with that of the Parisian maker Camus, who may have been a relative of the flautist. A recorder by Camus is listed in the Bruni Inventory of 1793 (*New Langwill*,).

## N 4

| | |
|---|---|
| MAKER | CAMUS |
| LOCATION | F – Paris: Musée de la Musique |
| COLLECTION NUMBER | E.980.2.102 |
| MATERIALS/MOUNTS | Ivory |
| PROVENANCE | ex Thibault de Chambure |
| SOURCES | Collection on-line catalogue: Lander |

*The Recorder In The Nineteenth Century*

Only the head of this recorder survives, the museum catalogue dating it as c1810. It is a small (sopranino or soprano) instrument.

|  |  |
|---|---|
|  | N 5 |
| MAKER | COLAS, Prosper |
| DATES | fl 1857 – p1883 |
| PLACE OF WORK | Paris (F) |
| LOCATION | US – MI – Ann Arbor: Stearns Collection |
| COLLECTION NUMBER | 503 |
| TYPE | Alto |
| LOWEST NOTE | a' |
| LENGTH | 392 mm |
| MATERIALS/MOUNTS | Box: rosewood beak to mouthpiece and terminal mount: horn ferrules |
| MARK | PROSPER COLAS/ A/ PARIS |
| SOURCES | Collection catalogue: Warner and von Huene (1970) |

Warner and von Huene comment on this recorder and A35 (together with an instrument by Kruspe, N21) as "coming from the nineteenth century when the instrument had regressed from artistic heights to become either a folk instrument or a toy".[16] The recorder is of a simple outline (with minimal bulges at the joints) and bears a marked similarity to the anonymous instruments A2, A6, A7, A34, and A35 and to the alto by F.Noblet (N45). The museum literature describes the recorder as a treble (modern term alto) but an instrument in a' would normally be called a third flute. *New Langwill* describes Colas as a maker of woodwind and brass instruments, a dealer, and maker of bows and glass mouthpieces for brass instruments.

|  |  |
|---|---|
|  | N 6 |
| MAKER | DUPRE, Pierre Paul Ghislain |
| DATES | 1790 – 1862 |
| PLACE OF WORK | Tournai (B) |
| LOCATION | B – Brussels: Musée des Instruments de Musique |
| COLLECTION NUMBER | M 2633 |
| TYPE | Alto |
| LOWEST NOTE | g' |
| MATERIALS/MOUNTS | Blackwood: 2 ivory rings |

---

16  Warner, R.A., von Huene, F., 'The Baroque Recorders in the Stearns Collection of Musical Instruments', *Galpin Society Journal* XXIII (1970), pp69-81

| | |
|---|---|
| KEYS | 2 |
| MARK | DUPRE a TOURNAI |
| SOURCES | De Keyser (personal communication 2003): Mahillon IV:[17] museum visit |

*New Langwill* gives that Dupré was "self-taught, [and] began with cane flutes". No other instruments by this maker are known.

N 7

| | |
|---|---|
| MAKER | GALPIN, Francis William |
| DATES | 1858 – 1945 |
| PLACE OF WORK | Hatfield Broad Oak (GB) |
| LOCATION | US – MA – Boston: Museum of Fine Arts |
| COLLECTION NUMBER | 17.1805 |
| TYPE | Alto |
| LOWEST NOTE | g' |
| LENGTH | 450 mm |
| MATERIALS/MOUNTS | Stained pear: 1 piece |
| PROVENANCE | ex Galpin: acquired by the museum in 1915-16 |
| SOURCES | Collection on-line catalogue: Bessaraboff[18] |

An alto of renaissance type. This instrument and the three following form a quartet (alto in g', tenor in d', basset in g, and bass in c – the pitches of the renaissance consort) and were exhibited at the Fishmonger's Hall Exhibition in 1904 and played in concerts at Hatfield Broad Oak in 1904 and 1905. They were built as playable reproductions of old instruments, having been finished by Galpin although the bodies of the instruments were made by woodwind instrument-making firms. The instruments are illustrated in Galpin's *Old English Instruments of Music* which was first published in 1910. Galpin's work and the history of these recorders is further discussed in Chapter IX 'The Revival of the Recorder'.

N 8

| | |
|---|---|
| MAKER | GALPIN, Francis William |
| LOCATION | US – MA – Boston: Museum of Fine Arts |
| COLLECTION NUMBER | 17.1806 |
| TYPE | Tenor |

---

17   Mahillon, V-C., *Catalogue descriptif et analytique du Musée Instrumental du Conservatoire Royale de Musique de Bruxelles*, (Ghent : Ad Hoste, 5 vols. 1893-1922)

18   Bessaraboff, N., *Ancient Musical Instruments: an Organological Study of the Musical Instruments in the Leslie Miller Mason Collection at the Museum of Fine Arts, Boston*, (Cambridge, Mass.: Harvard University Press 1941)

*The Recorder In The Nineteenth Century*

| | |
|---|---|
| LOWEST NOTE | d' |
| LENGTH | 643 mm |
| MATERIALS/MOUNTS | Stained pear |

    See notes on recorder N 7. Bessaraboff refers to this instrument as a 'tenor-alto' recorder, a term which derives from the seventeenth-century author and composer Michael Praetorius.

### N 9

| | |
|---|---|
| MAKER | GALPIN, Francis William |
| LOCATION | US – MA – Boston: Museum of Fine Arts |
| COLLECTION NUMBER | 17.1807 |
| TYPE | Basset |
| LOWEST NOTE | g |
| LENGTH | 921 mm |
| MATERIALS/MOUNTS | Stained walnut: fontanelle: brass ferrules |
| KEYS | 1 (double finger-touch lever) |

    See notes on recorder N 7. This instrument is a reproduction of a sixteenth century instrument in Galpin's collection. The fontanelle covering the key is typical of the larger renaissance recorders.

### N 10

| | |
|---|---|
| MAKER | GALPIN, Francis William |
| LOCATION | US – MA – Boston: Museum of Fine Arts |
| COLLECTION NUMBER | 17.1808 |
| TYPE | Bass |
| LOWEST NOTE | c |
| LENGTH | 1330 mm |
| MATERIALS/MOUNTS | Stained walnut: fontanelle: brass ferrules |
| KEYS | 1 (double finger-touch lever) |

    See notes on recorders N 7 - 9. This instrument is a reproduction of a type found at Verona, Brussels, Berlin, and Vienna (Bessaroff): it is blown with a crook.

### N 11

| | |
|---|---|
| MAKER | GARSI |
| DATES | fl 1812 – |
| PLACE OF WORK | Parma (I) |
| LOCATION | I – Parma: Conservatorio |

*Inventory of Recorders*

| | |
|---|---|
| TYPE | Bass |
| MARK | (sun)/ GARSI/ PARMA |
| SOURCE | *New Langwill* |

Garsi is also known as a maker of clarinets and bassoons. This is a very late example of a bass recorder: no other recorders by this maker have come to light.

N 12

| | |
|---|---|
| MAKER | GERLACH, Gottlieb Johann |
| DATES | 1856 – 1909  fl 1895 – 1909 |
| PLACE OF WORK | Munich (D) |
| LOCATION | D – Bavaria: secret private collection |
| TYPE | Alto |
| LOWEST NOTE | f' |
| MATERIALS/MOUNTS | Box: unmounted |
| SOURCES | Kirnbauer:[19] *New Langwill* |

This instrument is believed to be the earliest copy of a baroque recorder to be made in Germany in the early days of the recorder revival. It is a copy of an instrument by J.Denner, formerly in the possession of the Bogenhauser Künstlerkapelle (Chapter IX): although of poor playing quality, it is of considerable historical interest.

N 13

| | |
|---|---|
| MAKER | GOULDING & CO. |
| DATES | c1786 – 1834 |
| PLACE OF WORK | London (GB) |
| LOCATION | US – PA – Philadelphia: Oster (dealer) |
| TYPE | Alto |
| LENGTH | 470 mm |
| MATERIALS/MOUNTS | Box: unmounted |
| MARK | GOULDING & CO./ LONDON |
| SOURCES | Lander: Young |

The firm founded by Goulding in London around 1786 traded under several partnerships until 1834. Between the years 1798 and 1803 the company used the mark 'GOULDING & CO./ LONDON' while trading in St.James' Street and Pall Mall. The instrument is of very late eighteenth or very early nineteenth century origin, and exhibits the straight foot joint

---

[19] Kirnbauer, M., *Das war Pionierarbeit-Die Bogenhauser Künstlerkapelle, ein frühes Ensemble alte Musik*, in ed. Gutmann, V., *Alte Musik II: Konzert und Rezeption*, (Winterthur: Amadeus Verlag 1992), p62

## The Recorder In The Nineteenth Century

common on English recorders of the period: this was first seen on recorders by Thomas Stanesby, jr. (1692 – 1754). Examples of such a foot joint are found on a tenor recorder by Stanesby in F – Paris (Musée de la Musique, E 980.2.86), N14, N15, N49, and N56 in the present inventory.

### N 14

| | |
|---|---|
| MAKER | GOULDING & CO. |
| LOCATION | J – Tokyo – Iino: private collection |
| TYPE | Alto |
| LOWEST NOTE | g' (a' = 405) |
| LENGTH | 455 mm |
| MATERIALS/MOUNTS | Box: unmounted |
| MARK | GOULDING & CO./ LONDON/ 2 |
| SOURCES | Lander: Young |

This recorder has a straight foot joint.

### N 15

| | |
|---|---|
| MAKER | GOULDING & CO. |
| LOCATION | GB – London: Victoria and Albert Museum |
| COLLECTION NUMBER | 285 – 1882 |
| TYPE | Tenor |
| LENGTH | 660 mm |
| MATERIALS/MOUNTS | Box: unmounted |
| MARK | GOULDING & CO |
| SOURCES | Lander: museum catalogue: Young: museum visit |

Much has been written (often erroneously) about this unusual recorder which has a straight foot joint, the bore of which is slightly tapered unlike most transverse flutes of the period in which the bore was more commonly cylindrical.

The recorder has a beehive-shaped sponge chamber with a centre embouchure hole, and within this cap is a 14 mm space to contain a sponge to absorb the moisture from the player's breath in the manner of English flageolets of the period. As has been noted above (Chapter I) Charles Burney, travelling in Florence in 1770, heard a recorder played 'through a sponge'; it may be that Burney heard a flageolet rather than a true recorder, but this would seem improbable as Burney was a very knowledgeable man who would have known the difference between the two instruments. Two further instruments with sponge chambers are described below (D3, D5).

*Inventory of Recorders*

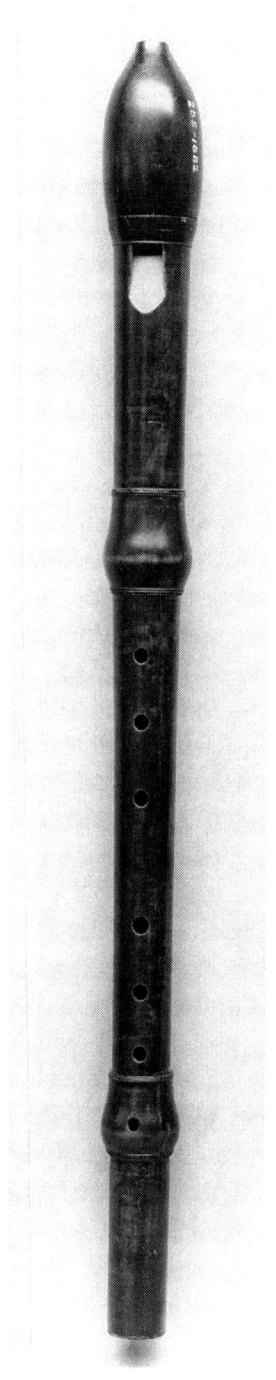

Tenor recorder by Goulding
N15
Reproduced by permission of the Victoria and Albert Museum, London

## The Recorder In The Nineteenth Century

A hole has been crudely pierced in the cap, the purpose of which appears to permit the attachment of a thin membrane to produce a buzzing sound when the instrument is played, mimicking the sound of the Chinese eunuch flute. The workmanship relating to this hole is of inferior quality, suggesting that it was carried out by an amateur subsequent to the instrument's manufacture. The membrane-covered hole is also found on Macgregor's 'Patent Voice Flute' of 1810, but this instrument was not a voice flute in the manner of a recorder in d' but a transverse alto flute. It is tempting to reflect that the owner of the Goulding tenor was attempting to produce a similar sound from his instrument.

In his *Popular Music of the Olden Times* (1855 – 1859) Chappell referred to the Goulding recorder, describing "Old English Flutes with a hole bored in the side, in the upper part of the instrument, the hole being covered with a piece of skin". Chappell surmised that "this would give somewhat the effect of the quill or reed of the hautboy, and these were called the recorder". It is difficult to ascertain whether Chappell believed this membrane to be called 'the recorder' or that all recorders possessed this feature. The instrument was but poorly understood at this time and it was not appreciated by Chappell that the membrane-covered hole on this particular recorder was exceptional (and probably unique).

The distinguished organologist Carl Engel owned the recorder in the mid- nineteenth century and considered it to be a seventeenth-century instrument on the grounds that it appeared similar to a recorder illustrated on the frontispiece to *The Genteel Companion*, a treatise for the recorder published in 1685. In 1874 Engel discussed the possible differences between the 'flûte à bec' and the recorder and appears to have believed that the significant difference was the possession, by the recorder, of the membrane-covered hole. Chappell, as noted above, concurred with this view. Welch, in the first of his six lectures, indicated that, far from being a seventeenth-century instrument, the maker's mark on the recorder dated it as being of early nineteenth-century origin.[20]

From this discussion, two strands emerge: the first is organological, and relates to the unusual features of the recorder, namely the sponge chamber (which is most unusual) and the membrane-covered hole (which appears to be unique). The first is an attempt to prevent the common problem of condensation in the windway by means of a device appropriated from the flageolet, the second an attempt by a player to alter the sound of the instrument. The second strand of the discussion is more significant and relates to the perception of the recorder in England in the latter half of the nineteenth century. That there was confusion about the characteristic features of the recorder is apparent from both Chappell's and Engel's remarks and indeed Engel observed in 1874 that few people would have seen a recorder as the instrument had become very scarce. What had been - and again is - a familiar instrument was only an historical curiosity with which the new science of organology had yet to engage.

---

20  Welch, C. *Six Lectures on the Recorder and other Flutes in relation to Literature*, (London: Oxford University Press 1911), pp103-127

*Inventory of Recorders*

Unfortunately the recorder is no longer in playing condition.

|  |  |
|---|---|
|  | N 16 |
| MAKER | GOULDING & CO. |
| LOCATION | US – NY – New York: Metropolitan Museum of Art |
| COLLECTION NUMBER | 1989.194.2 |
| TYPE | Alto |
| LOWEST NOTE | f' |
| LENGTH | 470 mm |
| MATERIALS/MOUNTS | Box |
| MARK | GOULDING & CO./LONDON |
| SOURCES | Heyde:[21] Lander |

The letters 'R W 1840' are scratched on the head of this recorder. Recorder N62 (by Lorenz Walch II) in Berchtesgaden bears a similar mark, but the significance of this is not known.

|  |  |
|---|---|
|  | N 17 |
| MAKER | GOULDING & CO. |
| LOCATION | D – Celle: Moeck (private collection) |
| TYPE | Alto |
| LOWEST NOTE | f' |
| MATERIALS/MOUNTS | Box |
| SOURCE | Haase-Moeck (personal communication) |

|  |  |
|---|---|
|  | N 18 |
| MAKER | GRAS, Charles |
| DATES | fl 1836 – a1892 |
| PLACE OF WORK | Paris (F) |
| LOCATION | F – Paris : Musée de la Musique |
| COLLECTION NUMBER | E 1457 |
| TYPE | Soprano |
| LENGTH | 362 mm |
| MATERIALS/MOUNTS | Ebony: ivory head and foot joints |
| MARK | (bird)/ GRAS |
| SOURCES | Collection on-line catalogue: Lander |

Charles Gras was a member of a long-established family firm (*New Langwill*). This author notes that there were a number of members of the family who bore the name

---

21    Heyde, H., personal communication 2002

'Charles'. As the recorder was purchased by the museum in 1893 it is likely that its maker is the Charles Gras cited above.

|  | N 19 |
|---|---|
| MAKER | HOCHSCHWARZER, A. |
| DATES | ?mid nineteenth century |
| PLACE OF WORK | Schwaz (A) |
| LOCATION | D – Sigmaringen: Schloss |
| MUSEUM NUMBER | 279/318 |
| TYPE | Fourth flute |
| LOWEST NOTE | b' |
| MARK | A.HOCHSCHWARZER/ SCHWAZ |
| SOURCES | Bär:[22] Lander: *New Langwill* |

*New Langwill* comments "A surviving recorder of folk instrument type resembles a similar instrument by Lorenz Walch". The present author considers it inappropriate to denigrate the Walch recorders as being of 'folk instrument type' but has not been able to study the Hochschwarzer instrument or further details thereof.

|  | N 20 |
|---|---|
| MAKER | JEANTET (?Jean) |
| DATES | fl a1823 – p1827 |
| PLACE OF WORK | Lyon (F) |
| LOCATION | F – Paris: Musée de la Musique |
| COLLECTION NUMBER | E 980.2.590 |
| LENGTH | c400 mm (head lost) |
| KEYS | 6 |
| MARK | JEANTET/ A LYON |
| PROVENANCE | ex Thibault de Chambure |
| SOURCES | Collection on-line catalogue: Lander |

The head of this recorder is missing: the length of the remaining pieces suggest that the instrument is a voice flute or a tenor. It is built in four pieces with a straight foot and six keys. The pattern of the keywork is quite different from that of a similarly-dated French recorder by Bellissent (N1).

*New Langwill* notes that Jeantet was listed as *facteur et marchand d'instruments*. No other recorders are extant but a small number of other woodwind instruments are preserved.

---

[22] Bär, F., Musikinstrumenten in Schloss Sigmaringen, *Tibia* 2 (1992), pp125-131

|  |  |
|---|---|
|  | N 21 |
| MAKER | KRUSPE, Franz-Carl |
| DATES | 1808 – 1885 (firm continued p1950) |
| PLACE OF WORK | Erfurt (D) |
| LOCATION | US – MI – Ann Arbor: Stearns Collection |
| COLLECTION NUMBER | 508 |
| TYPE | Treble beaked flute in A |
| LENGTH | 489 mm |
| MATERIALS/MOUNTS | Stained box: German silver ferrules: clarinet-like bell |
| KEYS | 4 nickel-plated |
| MARK | (lyre)/ KRUSPE/ ERFURT/ (wheel with six spokes) |
| SOURCES | Collection catalogue: Warner and von Huene (1970) |

This instrument is described by Warner and von Huene (1970) as "hardly a recorder in the normal sense but displays traits common to the English flageolet: a four-keyed beak flute": however, a photograph obtained from the museum displays a recorder-like instrument with a typical recorder 'beak' mouthpiece, seven finger holes and four keys. The appearances are much more characteristic of the recorder than the flageolet apart from the keywork, and it must be recalled that keywork on smaller recorders, although uncommon, is far from unknown in the nineteenth century. In modern terminology, the instrument would be called a third flute.

*New Langwill* relates that Kruspe worked in Mülhausen from 1829 to 1836, thereafter moving to Erfurt. He was an outstanding innovator, making many improvements to the transverse flute and other woodwind instruments.

|  |  |
|---|---|
|  | N 22 |
| MAKER | LAMY, Joseph Alfred |
| DATES | 1850 – 1919 |
| PLACE OF WORK | London (GB) |
| LOCATION | F – Paris : Musée de la Musique |
| COLLECTION NUMBER | E 01201 |
| TYPE | Soprano |
| SOURCE | Collection on-line catalogue |

The catalogue lists this instrument as being of nineteenth-century origin. Little is known of the maker save that he also made violin bows but a tenor recorder by a Lamy passed through Sotheby's Sale Rooms in New York in 1995. The maker could have been

Concord Lamy (fl mid C20) rather than Joseph Alfred: other recorders by this maker survive, but the present location of the 'Sotheby' Lamy is not known.

|  |  |
|---|---|
|  | N 23 |
| MAKER | LECOMTE, Arsène Zoë |
| DATES | 1818 – 1892 |
| PLACE OF WORK | Paris (F) |
| LOCATION | F – Paris: Sallaberry (private collection) |
| COLLECTION NUMBER | 1 |
| TYPE | Soprano |
| LOWEST NOTE | c" |
| LENGTH | 326 mm |
| MATERIALS/MOUNTS | Palisander: 1 nickel-silver ring: 2 pieces |
| MARK | A.LECOMTE & Cie./ PARIS |
| SOURCE | Collection catalogue |

The firm of Lecomte & Cie. was founded by Lecomte and flourished in Paris from 1859 to post-1910 (*New Langwill*). Information about this and the following recorder is taken from a catalogue of the collection published in special number XIV of *Larigot* 2003 (Journal of L'Association des Collectionneurs d'Instruments de Musique à Vent), a copy of which was supplied to the author in a personal communication from Gétreau (2003). The catalogue dates this and the following instrument as c1890.

|  |  |
|---|---|
|  | N 24 |
| MAKER | LECOMTE, Arsène Zoë |
| LOCATION | F – Paris: Sallaberry |
| COLLECTION NUMBER | 2 |
| TYPE | Soprano |
| LOWEST NOTE | c" |
| LENGTH | 325 mm |
| MATERIALS/MOUNTS | Palisander: 1 nickel-silver ring: 2 pieces |

See previous instrument.

|  |  |
|---|---|
|  | N 25 |
| MAKER | LÖHNER (LEHNER) Friedrich II |
| DATES | 1797 – 1865 |
| PLACE OF WORK | Nuremberg (D) |
| LOCATION | CH – Basel: Historisches Museum |

| | |
|---|---|
| COLLECTION NUMBER | 1896.199a |
| TYPE | Alto |
| LOWEST NOTE | f' |
| LENGTH | 500 mm |
| MATERIALS/MOUNTS | Box: unmounted |
| MARK | F.LEHNER/ FL |
| SOURCES | Gutmann (personal communication 2002): Lander: *New Langwill*: Nickel: museum visit |

    The nomenclature of the family Löhner has been studied by Nickel (1971).[23] Friedrich Löhner was born in 1737 and in 1762 became a master turner. He taught his craft to his son Johann Andreas (1768 – 1853: see recorders N 28, N 29), who was the father of Friedrich II (1797 – 1865). All three men worked in Nuremberg using different marks, and some confusion has arisen with regard to the ascription of surviving recorders (and other instruments) to particular members of the family. Nickel's study elucidates the matter.

    Friedrich Löhner I's mark is given as (fleur-de-lys)/ F. LÖHNER/ A/ NURNBERG whereas Nickel ascribes the mark (fleur-de-lys)/ F.LEHNER/ FL (monogram) to Friedrich II. The recorder under discussion bears the mark F.LEHNER/ FL on all three joints and according to Nickel's work is therefore a nineteenth-century instrument by Friedrich II. *New Langwill*, however, suggests that some of the instruments (not necessarily the recorders) bearing this mark may be of earlier manufacture.

    A catalogue of the Basel collection published in 1906 notes that both this and the following recorder were used in church services in Adelboden (Switzerland).

N 26
| | |
|---|---|
| MAKER | LÖHNER (LEHNER) Friedrich II |
| LOCATION | CH – Basel: Historisches Museum |
| COLLECTION NUMBER | 1896.199b |

    This recorder is identical to N 25.

N 27
| | |
|---|---|
| MAKER | LÖHNER, Johann Andreas |
| DATES | 1768 – 1853 |
| PLACE OF WORK | Nuremberg (D) |
| LOCATION | D – Erlangen: Universität |
| COLLECTION NUMBER | R 24 |

---

23  Nickel, E., *Der Holzblasinstrumenten in der freien Riechsstadt Nürnberg*, (Munich: Musikverlag Emil Katzbichler 1971), pp313-314

| | |
|---|---|
| TYPE | Alto |
| LOWEST NOTE | g' |
| LENGTH | 493 mm |
| MARK | (tree)/ J.A.LÖHNER/ A/ NURNBERG |
| SOURCES | Eschler[24]: Lander: *New Langwill* |

The foot of this instrument is of early nineteenth-century manufacture: the upper joints may be very late eighteenth century (Eschler). For biographical information see the notes to recorder N25.

N 28

| | |
|---|---|
| MAKER | LÖHNER, J.A. |
| LOCATION | S – Stockholm: Musikmuseet |
| COLLECTION NUMBER | F 174 |
| TYPE | Alto |
| MARK | (tree)/ J.A.LÖHNER [cursive]/ A/ NURNBERG [cursive]/ (two stars) |
| SOURCES | Eastop (personal communication 2003): Lander |

N 29

| | |
|---|---|
| MAKER | MAHILLON, Victor-Charles |
| DATES | 1841 – 1924 |
| PLACE OF WORK | Brussels (B) |
| LOCATION | I – Florence: Conservatorio |
| MUSEUM NUMBER | 107 |
| TYPE | Tenor |
| LENGTH | 596 mm |
| SOURCE | Collection catalogue |

This instrument is a renaissance-style *flûte à neuf trous* and is described in the catalogue as a very accurate copy of a renaissance recorder. Like the following instrument, it was made in the workshop of Mahillon in Brussels and given to the Florentine museum in perpetuity.

The firm of Mahillon was founded by Charles Borromée Mahillon (1813 – 1887): his eldest son, Victor-Charles, joined the firm in 1865 and was responsible for commissioning copies of historic instruments, some of which were used in performance. It is open to question whether Mahillon himself made the instruments but his contributions both to

---

24  Eschler, T.J., 'The Collection of Historical Musical Instruments of the University of Erlangen', *Galpin Society Journal* XXXVI (1983), pp115-121

organology and to the revival of the recorder were considerable and are discussed in Chapter IX.

|  |  |
|---|---|
|  | N 30 |
| MAKER | MAHILLON, Victor-Charles |
| LOCATION | I – Florence: Conservatorio |
| COLLECTION NUMBER | 108 |
| TYPE | Bass (basset) |
| LENGTH | 975 mm |
| MATERIALS/MOUNTS | Ebony: ivory mounts |
| KEYS | 1 swallow key |
| SOURCE | Collection catalogue |

This recorder is in the baroque style and is blown through a crook.

|  |  |
|---|---|
|  | N 31 |
| MAKER | MAHILLON, Victor-Charles |
| LOCATION | B – Brussels: Musée des Instruments de Musique |
| COLLECTION NUMBER | 1023 |
| TYPE | Sopranino |
| LOWEST NOTE | g" |
| SOURCES | Mahillon II : museum visit |

This instrument is one of a set of eight recorders copied from instruments by Kynseker (1636 – 1686) in the Germanisches Nationalmuseum in Nuremberg. The copies are of considerable interest as they were played in London at the International Inventions Exhibition in 1885 and displayed again in London at the Royal Military Exhibition in 1890. The instruments are well made and remain in good condition in a leather case.

The remainder of the set is listed on the following pages: the pitch notation (g and d) was common in the renaissance. There is one sopranino, two each of soprano, alto, and tenor, and one basset.

This set comprises N31 to N38: each instrument is listed separately, although they all are catalogued as 1023 in the collection.

|  |  |
|---|---|
|  | N 32 |
| MAKER | MAHILLON, Victor-Charles |
| LOCATION | B – Brussels: Musée des Instruments de Musique |
| COLLECTION NUMBER | 1023 |
| TYPE | Soprano |

LOWEST NOTE                    d"

   One of a set of eight.

                                N 33
MAKER                          MAHILLON, Victor –Charles
LOCATION                       B – Brussels: Musée des Instruments de Musique
COLLECTION NUMBER              1023
TYPE                           Soprano
LOWEST NOTE                    d"

   One of a set of eight.

                                N 34
MAKER                          MAHILLON, Victor-Charles
LOCATION                       B – Brussels: Musée des Instruments de Musique
COLLECTION NUMBER              1023
TYPE                           Alto
LOWEST NOTE                    g'

   One of a set of eight.

                                N 35
MAKER                          MAHILLON, Victor-Charles
LOCATION                       B – Brussels: Musée des Instruments de Musique
COLLECTION NUMBER              1023
TYPE                           Alto
LOWEST NOTE                    g'

   One of a set of eight.

                                N 36
MAKER                          MAHILLON, Victor-Charles
LOCATION                       B – Brussels: Musée des Instruments de Musique
COLLECTION NUMBER              1023
TYPE                           Tenor
LOWEST NOTE                    d'

   One of a set of eight.

|  |  |
|---|---|
|  | N 37 |
| MAKER | MAHILLON, Victor-Charles |
| LOCATION | B – Brussels: Musée des Instruments de Musique |
| COLLECTION NUMBER | 1023 |
| TYPE | Tenor |
| LOWEST NOTE | d' |

One of a set of eight.

|  |  |
|---|---|
|  | N 38 |
| MAKER | MAHILLON, Victor-Charles |
| LOCATION | B – Brussels: Musée des Instruments de Musique |
| COLLECTION NUMBER | 1023 |
| TYPE | Basset |
| LOWEST NOTE | g |

One of a set of eight.

|  |  |
|---|---|
|  | N 39 |
| MAKER | MAHILLON, Victor-Charles |
| LOCATION | B – Brussels: Musée des instruments de Musique |
| COLLECTION NUMBER | 1029 |
| TYPE | Bass |
| LOWEST NOTE | c |
| LENGTH | 1360 mm |
| KEYS | 1 |
| SOURCE | Mahillon II |

A renaissance-style bass recorder with a fontanelle: it is a copy of an instrument in the Municipal Museum of Verona.

|  |  |
|---|---|
|  | N 40 |
| MAKER | MAHILLON, Victor-Charles |
| LOCATION | B – Brussels: Musée des Instruments de Musique |
| COLLECTION NUMBER | 1030 |
| TYPE | Bass |
| LOWEST NOTE | ? a flat |
| LENGTH | 1760 mm |
| KEYS | 4 |

## The Recorder In The Nineteenth Century

MARK                          Hans Rauch von Schratt
SOURCE                 Mahillon II

A renaissance-style bass recorder which is a copy of an instrument in Le Musée National de Musique (now the Bavarian National Museum) in Munich. Rauch was a member of a significant family of woodwind instrument makers which flourished in Shrattenbach in the late fifteenth and early sixteenth centuries (*New Langwill*).

According to *New Langwill* Rauch did not use his name *only* as a mark and the simple inscription 'Hans Rauch von Schratt' is most likely of Mahillon's invention. A similar confusion is demonstrated in recorders A38 – A40.

                                     N 41
MAKER                         MAHILLON, Victor-Charles
LOCATION                 B – Brussels: Musée des Instruments de Musique
COLLECTION NUMBER    1035
TYPE                             Contrabass
LOWEST NOTE             D
LENGTH                       2620 mm
KEYS                             4
SOURCE                       Mahillon II

This very large recorder is a copy of a renaissance-style instrument in Le Musée du Steen (now the Vleeshuis Museum) in Antwerp, and was brought to London for the Royal Military Exhibition in 1890. A further (anonymous) copy of a contrabass from Antwerp is listed as A43 but it measures only 2602 mm. The catalogue of the Antwerp collection states that Mahillon caused two copies of the instrument to be made in 1881, and that one copy (the present instrument) is in Brussels, the other (possibly A43) being given to the Crosby Brown Collection in New York.[25] If this is indeed the case, it is surprising that the two copies are of dissimilar length.

                                      N 42
MAKER                         MAHILLON, Victor-Charles
LOCATION                 B – Brussels: Musée des Instruments de Musique
COLLECTION NUMBER    1041
TYPE                             Basset
LOWEST NOTE             g
LENGTH                       920 mm

---

25   *Catalogus van de Muziekinstrumenten uit de Versameling van heet Museum Vleeshuis*, (Antwerp: Ruckers Genootschap, 1981), p57

| | |
|---|---|
| KEYS | 2 |
| SOURCE | Mahillon II |

A baroque-style bass recorder, a copy of an instrument in Le Musée du Château at Darnstadt. A further baroque-style bass(et) is preserved in Florence (N30) but is 55 mm shorter: its fundamental is not known.

| | N 43 |
|---|---|
| MAKER | MARTIN, Jean-Baptiste |
| DATES | 1862 – 1923 |
| PLACE OF WORK | La Couture-Boussey (F) |
| LOCATION | F – Paris: Musée de la Musique |
| COLLECTION NUMBER | E 980.2.529 |
| TYPE | Tenor |
| MATERIALS/MOUNTS | Ivory mounts |
| KEYS | 1 swallow key |
| PROVENANCE | ex Thibault de Chambure |
| SOURCES | Collection on-line catalogue: Lander |

The collection catalogue states that the recorder was built in 1879 by Jean-Baptiste Martin of La Couture-Boussey. A dynasty of woodwind instrument makers by the name of Martin existed in La Couture from the middle of the eighteenth century, culminating in the formation of the firm Martin frères which flourished in Paris from c1840 to 1927: four members of the family bore the name Jean-Baptiste. The eldest Jean-Baptiste was born in 1751/2, Jean-Baptiste II lived from 1791 until 1867, Jean-Baptiste III from 1817 to 1877, with François Jean-Baptiste (1862 – 1923) being the last to bear the name (*New Langwill*). If the recorder was indeed made in 1879 (see below) the last-named would have been its maker: the instrument is similar in outward appearance to other French recorders of the late nineteenth century, a number of these also having a swallow key for the little finger. This may be the recorder referred to by Hunt, discovered when he visited the collection of Mme. Thibault de Chambure:

> I came across a tenor, obviously copied from an old one, on the butterfly key of which I read the following: "P.R. Souvenir de Couture 1875", and on the head of this very fine instrument "J.B.Martin à son ami Paul Roche".[26]

---

26  Hunt, E.H., *The Recorder and its Music*, (Hebden Bridge: Peacock Press, 3rd ed., 2002), p144

*The Recorder In The Nineteenth Century*

|  |  |
|---|---|
|  | N 44 |
| MAKER | MARTIN, Johann Gottfried |
| DATES | c1772 – p1842 |
| PLACE OF WORK | Potsdam (D) |
| LOCATION | D – Leipzig: Universität |
| COLLECTION NUMBER | 1146 |
| TYPE | Bassett |
| LOWEST NOTE | f |
| LENGTH | 962 mm |
| MATERIALS/MOUNTS | Maple: ivory mounts |
| KEYS | 4 |
| MARK | Prussian eagle/ MARTIN/ POTSDAM |
| SOURCES | Lander: collection catalogue: *New Langwill* |

Heyde (compiler of the catalogue) considers this to be one of the last 'bass recorders' to have been built before the recorder's decline. It is blown with a crook: four keys on a basset recorder are unremarkable.

|  |  |
|---|---|
|  | N45 |
| MAKER | NOBLET, F. |
| DATES | c1820 |
| PLACE OF WORK | Paris |
| LOCATION | GB – Oxford: Bate Collection |
| MUSEUM NUMBER | 0405 |
| TYPE | Alto |
| LENGTH | 486 mm |
| MATERIALS/MOUNTS | Box: horn mouthpiece, rings, and bell rim |
| MAKER'S MARK | (cockerel)/F.NOBLET/(star) |
| SOURCE | Bingham[27] |

This instrument was offered for sale by Bingham in early 2005. The recorder is in good condition except for some damage to the horn lip which does not effect playing. The appearance of the instrument (as illustrated on Bingham's website) is very similar to the recorder by Colas (N5) and the anonymous French instruments A2, A6, A7, A34 and A35.

*New Langwill* notes that the Noblet family was large, with inter-relationships being unclear. Family members worked in La Couture-Boussey, Ivry-la-Bataille and Paris. The date '*circa* mid C19' is given for F. Noblet.

---

27   www.oldmusicalinstruments.co.uk

*Inventory of Recorders*

|  |  |
|---|---|
|  | N 46 |
| MAKER | NOBLET ET THIBOUVILLE |
| DATES | fl1862 – 1887 |
| PLACE OF WORK | Ivry-la-Bataille (F) |
| LOCATION | xD – Berlin: Institut für Musikforschung |
| COLLECTION NUMBER | x2905 |
| SOURCES | *Langwill (1977)* Wittenbrink (personal communication 2002) |

A personal communication from Bernd Wittenbrink, museum curator, advised that both this and the following instrument were lost in the Second World War. Neither photographs nor documentation have survived. The firm of Noblet et Thibouville was founded in 1862 with the union of a member of the woodwind-making family of Noblet with Eugène Thibouville.

|  |  |
|---|---|
|  | N 47 |
| MAKER | NOBLET ET THIBOUVILLE |
| LOCATION | xD – Berlin: Institut für Musikforschung |
| COLLECTION NUMBER | x2983 |

See previous instrument.

|  |  |
|---|---|
|  | N 48 |
| MAKER | NOBLET ET THIBOUVILLE |
| LOCATION | D – Celle : Moeck (private collection) |
| TYPE | Third flute |
| MATERIALS/MOUNTS | Box |
| SOURCE | Haase-Moeck (personal communication 2003) |

|  |  |
|---|---|
|  | N 49 |
| MAKER | OPPENHEIM |
| DATES | ?first half C19 |
| PLACE OF WORK | London (GB) |
| LOCATION | GB – Oxford: Bate Collection |
| COLLECTION NUMBER | 0404 |
| TYPE | ?Tenor |
| LENGTH | 542 mm |
| MARK | Oppenheim, London |
| SOURCE | la Rue (personal communication 2004) |

*The Recorder In The Nineteenth Century*

This instrument was recently acquired by the Bate Collection from Bingham. It has a straight flute-like foot-joint in common with many English recorders of the period. *New Langwill* lists 'Oppenheim' as a London woodwind instrument maker and 'M.Oppenheim' as also working in London: a firm of 'Oppenheim Brothers' flourished between 1876 and 1884.

|  |  |
|---|---|
|  | N 50 |
| MAKER | SCHIN |
| DATES | c1840 |
| PLACE OF WORK | Neuburg (D) |
| LOCATION | D – Nuremberg: Germanisches Nationalmuseum |
| COLLECTION NUMBER | MIR 197 |
| TYPE | Sixth flute |
| LOWEST NOTE | d" |
| LENGTH | 320 mm |
| MATERIALS/MOUNTS | Box: horn mounts |
| MARK | Schin, Neuburg: D (on body) |
| PROVENANCE | ex Ruck |
| SOURCES | Lander: collection on-line inventory; *New Langwill*: van der Meer (personal communication 1981) |

The workshop of Schin was founded by Joseph Schin I in the early nineteenth century and continued as a family concern until c1870. The collection inventory suggests a date of 1840 for this recorder. The letter 'D' appears on the body of the instrument: such marks indicating pitch are often found on Bavarian and Austrian instruments, in some cases being incorporated into the maker's mark.

|  |  |
|---|---|
|  | N 52 |
| MAKER | SCHWEFFER, Heinrich |
| DATES | c1814 – 1887 |
| PLACE OF WORK | Graz (A) |
| LOCATION | A – Graz: Landesmuseum Johanneum |
| COLLECTION NUMBER | KGW 1.423 |
| TYPE | Sixth flute |
| LOWEST NOTE | d" |
| LENGTH | 288 mm |
| MATERIALS/MOUNTS | Plum: foot joint of box |

*Inventory of Recorders*

| | |
|---|---|
| KEYS | 1 |
| MARK | SCHWEFFER/ GRAZ/ D |
| SOURCE | Collection catalogue |

The firm of Schweffer was established by Heinrich Schweffer, who was succeeded by his son August (1850 – 1940). The firm made other woodwind instruments including csakans. The letter 'D' in the mark is a pitch mark.

N 52

| | |
|---|---|
| MAKER | SCHWEFFER, Heinrich (workshop) |
| LOCATION | A – Graz: Landesmuseum Johanneum |
| COLLECTION NUMBER | KGW 1.422 |
| TYPE | Sixth flute |
| LOWEST NOTE | d" |
| LENGTH | 293 mm |
| MATERIALS/MOUNTS | Plum |
| SOURCE | Collection catalogue. |

The instrument is described as 'without beak' in the catalogue: it may represent a 'folk' recorder. A further recorder made in Graz 'without beak' but of anonymous origin is listed as A32.

N 54

| | |
|---|---|
| MAKER | THIBOUVILLE – CABART (workshop) |
| DATES | c1890 – 1901 |
| PLACE OF WORK | Paris (F) |
| LOCATION | D – Leipzig: Universität |
| COLLECTION NUMBER | 1114 |
| TYPE | Exilent |
| LOWEST NOTE | g" |
| LENGTH | 263 mm |
| MATERIALS/MOUNTS | Maple |
| SOURCE | Collection catalogue |

The instrument is described as a copy of an older style of recorder similar to those by Schlegel in Basel and Walch in Berchtesgaden (both these instruments are of the baroque type – author): it is a "simple and cheap" instrument. Heyde (author of the catalogue) also notes that the instrument is in the form of the lost Noblet et Thibouville recorders (N 46, N 47) which were located in Berlin. The catalogue gives 1890 – 1901 as the period of

## The Recorder In The Nineteenth Century

manufacture. *New Langwill* states that the firm of Thibouville-Cabart flourished in Ezy from about 1865, moving to Paris before 1875.

|  | N 54 |
|---|---|
| MAKER | THIBOUVILLE – CABART |
| LOCATION | I – Milan: Museo Castello Sforzesco |
| COLLECTION NUMBER | 318 |
| TYPE | Soprano |
| LENGTH | 320 mm |
| MATERIALS/MOUNTS | Box: ?horn mounts |
| MARK | THIBOUVILLE/ Cabart/ à Paris |
| SOURCE | Collection catalogue |

The catalogue dates this instrument as eighteenth century but this is clearly a mistake for the firm of Thibouville - Cabart was not founded until around 1865 (see N53).

|  | N 55 |
|---|---|
| MAKER | TOLBECQUE, Auguste |
| DATES | 1830 – 1919 |
| PLACE OF WORK | Niort (F) |
| LOCATION | F – Paris: Musée de la Musique |
| COLLECTION NUMBER | E 2138 |
| TYPE | Tenor (*quinte*) |
| LOWEST NOTE | d' |
| LENGTH | 715 mm |
| MATERIALS/MOUNTS | Stained box: 1 ivory ring and bell trim |
| KEYS | 1 |
| PROVENANCE | ex Cesbron: donated to museum in 1934 |
| SOURCES | Collection on-line catalogue: Lander |

This instrument is described in Cesbron's catalogue as a copy of a tenor recorder by Hotteterre in the same collection (E 590.2.0001). Technically, a recorder in d' would now be referred to as a voice flute, but the word *quinte* is best translated as 'tenor'.

Tolbecque was a 'cellist by training but in retirement built copies of old instruments.

|  | N 56 |
|---|---|
| MAKER | TOWNSEND |
| DATES | fl c1816 – c1869 |
| PLACE OF WORK | Manchester (GB) |

*Inventory of Recorders*

| | |
|---|---|
| LOCATION | Unknown: sold by auction 1990 |
| TYPE | ? sixth flute |
| MARK | 6/ Townsend/ ManchR |
| SOURCES | Blanchfield:[28] Lander |

This small recorder has the straight foot-joint common on English recorders of the period but the workmanship of the windway is of poor quality. It is likely that the figure '6' in the mark refers to the instrument being a sixth flute, this not appearing on other marks used by this maker, and is therefore analogous to the 'letter' pitch-marks used on the Bavarian and Austrian recorders. The instrument is well-worn, and appears to have been much used.

The firm of Townsend flourished in Manchester between c1825 and 1860 as music publishers, sellers, and instrument dealers. *New Langwill* gives the dates 1819 – 1869.

N 57

| | |
|---|---|
| MAKER | WALCH, Lorenz II |
| DATES | fl a1809 – 1862 |
| PLACE OF WORK | Berchtesgaden (D) |
| LOCATION | D – Munich: Deutsches Museum |
| COLLECTION NUMBER | 25961 |
| TYPE | Sixth flute |
| LOWEST NOTE | d" |
| LENGTH | 300 mm |
| MATERIALS/MOUNTS | Plum: unmounted |
| MARK | LORENZ/ WALCH/ BERCHTESGADEN/ D |
| SOURCES | Lander: collection catalogue: Young |

A Berchtesgadner Fleitl (Berchtesgaden small flute). The 'D' in the maker's mark is a pitch mark, and the museum catalogue describes the recorder as a 'folk-lore instrument'. The Berchtesgadener Fleitl and the Walch family are discussed subsequently in Chapter V, 'The Berchtesgadner Fleitl'.

N 58

| | |
|---|---|
| MAKER | WALCH, Lorenz II |
| LOCATION | A – Salzburg: Museo Carolino Augusteum |
| COLLECTION NUMBER | 3/3 |
| TYPE | Soprano |
| LOWEST NOTE | c" |

---

28  Blanchfield, D., 'A Nineteenth-Century English Recorder', *The Recorder Magazine* X 2 (1990), pp55-56

## The Recorder In The Nineteenth Century

LENGTH                              335 mm
MATERIALS/MOUNTS      Box: horn rings
MARK                                C/ LORENZ WALCH/ BERCHTESGADEN
SOURCE                            Lander: *New Langwill*: Young: museum visit

The author was permitted to play this instrument by courtesy of the Curator, Dr. Kurt Birsak, in October 2002. It is a high-quality recorder having a bright, clear tone and a compass of two octaves with good intonation. Marvin played this recorder whilst researching his 1972 paper 'Recorders and English Flutes in European Collections' and assessed the playability and tone of the recorder as 'fairly good'.[29]

The pitch mark 'C' is shown below

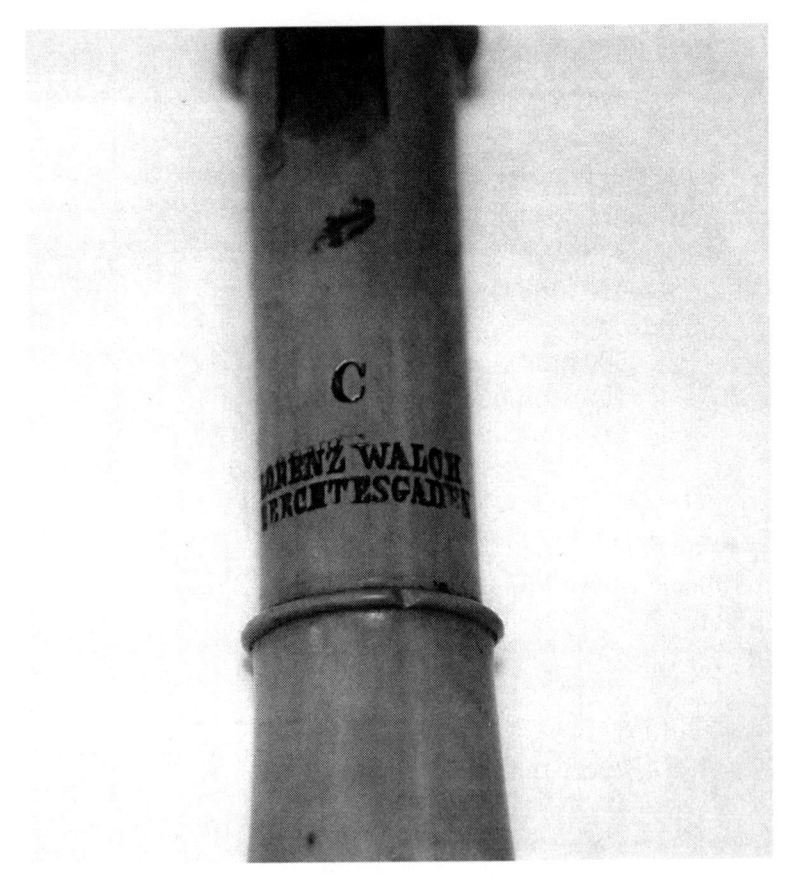

Pitch mark 'C' on recorder
by Lorenz Walch II
N58
Author's photograph

---

29   Marvin, B.,'Recorders and English Flutes in European Collections', *Galpin Society Journal* XXV (1972), pp30-57

|  |  |
|---|---|
|  | N 59 |
| MAKER | WALCH, Lorenz II |
| LOCATION | US – DC – Washington: DCM |
| COLLECTION NUMBER | 0663 |
| TYPE | Soprano |
| LOWEST NOTE | c" |
| LENGTH | 341 mm |
| MATERIALS/MOUNTS | Box: 2 horn rings |
| MARK | (5 petal flower)/ LORENZ WALCH/ BERCHTESGADEN/C |
| PROVENANCE | Bought from Koch (Munich) 1926 |
| SOURCES | Collection on-line catalogue: Lander: Young |

The characteristic form of the Berchtesgadner Fleitl is seen in the illustration of this instrument.

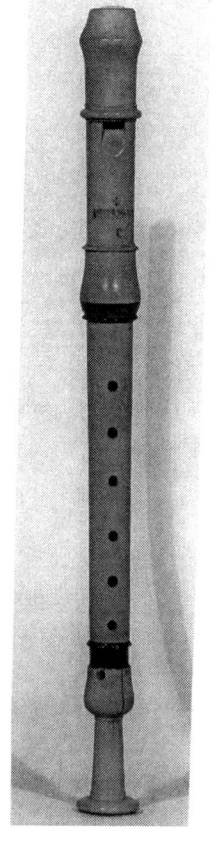

Soprano recorder by
Lorenz Walch II
N59
Reproduced by permission
of The Dayton C. Miller
Flute Collection

*The Recorder In The Nineteenth Century*

|  |  |
|---|---|
|  | N 60 |
| MAKER | WALCH, Lorenz II |
| LOCATION | D – Bonn: Beethovenhaus |
| COLLECTION NUMBER | 8 |
| TYPE | ?Soprano |
| LOWEST NOTE | ?c" |
| LENGTH | 300 mm |
| MATERIALS/MOUNTS | Plum: unmounted |
| MARK | (5 petal flower)/ LORENZ WALCH/ BERCHTESGADEN/ D |
| SOURCES | Lander: Young |

Young gives c" as the lowest note of this instrument but the recorder is stamped 'D' suggesting that it is not a soprano (fifth flute) but a sixth flute. The instrument measures 300 mm, which makes it likely that it is indeed a sixth flute, the two other fifth flutes by this maker (N58, N59) measuring 335 and 341 mm respectively, and the sixth flute (N57) 300 mm.

|  |  |
|---|---|
|  | N 61 |
| MAKER | WALCH, Lorenz II |
| LOCATION | D – Berchtesgaden: Heimatmuseum |
| COLLECTION NUMBER | 1074 |
| TYPE | Soprano |
| LOWEST NOTE | c" |
| LENGTH | 338 mm |
| MATERIALS/MOUNTS | Palisander: ivory mounts |
| MARK | C (pitch mark) |
| SOURCES | Bruckner:[30] Lander: Young: museum visit |

Young lists three soprano recorders by this maker in the Heimatmuseum in Berchtesgaden, but Bruckner's study of the Walch family lists only two (the present instrument and a third flute, N62). A visit to the museum by the present author in October 2002 confirmed Bruckner's observations.

|  |  |
|---|---|
|  | N 62 |
| MAKER | WALCH, Lorenz II |
| LOCATION | D – Berchtesgaden: Heimatmuseum |
| COLLECTION NUMBER | 1079 |

---

[30] Bruckner, H., 'Die Pfeifenmacher Walch in Berchtesgaden', *Sänger und Musiktanzenzeitung* 2 (1978), pp55-66

| | |
|---|---|
| TYPE | Third flute |
| LOWEST NOTE | a' flat |
| LENGTH | 419 mm |
| MATERIALS/MOUNTS | Plum: unmounted |
| MARK | LORENZ WALCH/ BERCHTESGADEN |
| SOURCES | Bruckner: Lander: Young: museum visit |

This recorder bears the mark 'RW' on the head, a similar mark being found on an alto by Goulding in the Metropolitan Museum of Art, New York (N16). The maker's mark is difficult to read but appears to bear the letter 'A' (indicating pitch) and a clover leaf as well as the above inscription. This is compatible with Lorenz Walch II's work.

### N 63

| | |
|---|---|
| MAKER | WALCH, Lorenz II |
| LOCATION | D – Stuttgart: Hase (private collection) |
| TYPE | Soprano |
| SOURCE | Young |

### N 64

| | |
|---|---|
| MAKER | WALCH, Lorenz II |
| LOCATION | D – Nuremberg: Germanisches Nationalmuseum |
| COLLECTION NUMBER | MIR 194 |
| TYPE | Soprano |
| LOWEST NOTE | c" |
| LENGTH | 340 mm |
| MATERIALS/MOUNTS | Plum |
| MARK | (flower)/ LORENZ WALCH/ BERCHTESGADEN |
| PROVENANCE | ex Rück |
| SOURCES | Lander: collection on-line inventory: van der Meer (personal communication 1981): Young |

The museum literature dates this instrument as c1855.

### N 65

| | |
|---|---|
| MAKER | WALCH, Paul |
| DATES | fl a1862 – 1873 |
| PLACE OF WORK | Berchtesgaden |
| LOCATION | A – Salzburg: Museo Carolino Augusteum |
| COLLECTION NUMBER | 3/1 |

| | |
|---|---|
| TYPE | Sixth flute |
| LOWEST NOTE | d" |
| LENGTH | 300 mm |
| MATERIALS/MOUNTS | Rosewood: ivory mounts |
| MARK | (8 petal flower)/ PAUL WALCH/ BERCHTESGADEN/ D |
| SOURCES | Lander: *New Langwill*: Young: museum visit |

The author was permitted to sound this instrument in October 2002: it is not in good condition but the tone is bright and similar to the soprano by Lorenz Walch II in the same collection (N58). Marvin (1972) commented that the playability and tone of the instrument were 'fairly good' (see also N58).

Biographical details of Paul Walch are given in Chapter V 'The Berchtesgadner Fleitl'.

### N 66

| | |
|---|---|
| MAKER | WALCH, Paul |
| LOCATION | D – Nuremberg: Germanisches Nationalmuseum |
| COLLECTION NUMBER | MIR 195 |
| TYPE | Soprano |
| LOWEST NOTE | c" |
| LENGTH | 336 mm |
| MATERIALS/MOUNTS | Box: horn mounts |
| MARK | (flower)/ PAUL WALCH/ BERCHTESGADEN/ C |
| SOURCES | Lander: collection on-line inventory: van der Meer (personal communication 1981): Young |

### N 67

| | |
|---|---|
| MAKER | WALCH, Paul |
| LOCATION | D – Nuremberg: Germanisches Nationalmuseum |
| COLLECTION NUMBER | MIR 196 |
| TYPE | Soprano |
| LOWEST NOTE | c" |
| LENGTH | 338 mm |
| MATERIALS/MOUNTS | Box: horn mounts |
| MARK | (flower)/ PAUL WALCH/ BERCHTESGADEN/ C |
| SOURCES | Lander: museum on-line inventory: van der Meer (personal communication 1981) Young |

Similar to N 66.

## N 68

| | |
|---|---|
| MAKER | WALCH, Paul |
| LOCATION | D – Bremen: Müller (private collection) |
| TYPE | Soprano |
| LOWEST NOTE | c" |
| LENGTH | 334 mm |
| MATERIALS/MOUNTS | Box: horn mounts |
| SOURCES | Lander: Young |

## A 1

| | |
|---|---|
| ORIGIN | Europe ?France |
| LOCATION | F – Paris: Musée de la Musique |
| COLLECTION NUMBER | E 980.2.542 |
| TYPE | Tenor |
| LENGTH | 710 mm |
| MATERIALS/MOUNTS | Palisander: ivory mounts and bell-rim |
| PROVENANCE | ex Thibault de Chambure |
| SOURCES | Collection on-line catalogue: Lander |

The recorder is of baroque pattern.

## A 2

| | |
|---|---|
| ORIGIN | ?France |
| LOCATION | F – Paris : Musée de la Musique |
| COLLECTION NUMBER | E 980.2.543 |
| TYPE | Alto |
| LENGTH | 460 mm |
| PROVENANCE | ex Thibault de Chambure |
| SOURCES | Collection catalogue: Lander |

The instrument is of a very plain outline, with only small bulges at the joints in contrast to the prominent bulges found on most baroque-style recorders. It bears a marked external similarity to E 980.2.555/556 (A6, A7) and also to anonymous recorders in Brussels (A34) and in the Stearns Collection in Ann Arbor (A35): a further instrument of like pattern is illustrated in Hipkin's *Musical Instruments Historic, Rare, and Unique* of 1888 but its present location is not known: it was formerly in the Glen Collection in Edinburgh. A recorder by Colas (c1857 – 1883) is also preserved in the Stearns Collection (N5) and appears externally identical to the above instruments: another recorder of similar appearance by Noblet (c1820) may be found in the Bate Collection on Oxford. I conclude that all these instruments are most probably Parisian and mostly date from the earliest days of the recorder revival.

### A 3

| | |
|---|---|
| ORIGIN | Europe ?France |
| LOCATION | F – Paris : Musée de la Musique |
| COLLECTION NUMBER | E 980.2.545 |
| TYPE | Alto |
| LENGTH | 505 mm |
| MATERIALS/MOUNTS : | Ebony |
| PROVENANCE | ex Thibault de Chambure |
| SOURCES | Collection on-line catalogue: Lander |

The recorder is of baroque pattern.

### A 4

| | |
|---|---|
| ORIGIN | Europe ? France |
| LOCATION | F – Paris : Musée de la Musique |
| COLLECTION NUMBER | E 980.2.546 |
| TYPE | Alto |
| LENGTH | 545 mm |
| PROVENANCE | ex Thibault de Chambure |
| SOURCES | Collection on-line catalogue: Lander |

Lander comments that the foot-joint may not be original: the instrument is otherwise similar to A 3.

### A 5

| | |
|---|---|
| ORIGIN | Europe ?France |
| LOCATION | F – Paris: Musée de la Musique |
| COLLECTION NUMBER | E 980.2.547 |
| TYPE | Alto |
| LENGTH | c650 mm |
| MATERIALS/MOUNTS | Ivory beak |
| KEYS | 1 swallow key |
| PROVENANCE | ex Thibault de Chambure |
| SOURCES | Collection on-line catalogue: Lander |

Although this instrument is described as an alto, its size suggests that it is more likely to be a voice flute or tenor recorder. The lowest note is not given.

*Inventory of Recorders*

|  | A 6 |
|---|---|
| ORIGIN | Europe ?France |
| LOCATION | F – Paris: Musée de la Musique |
| COLLECTION NUMBER | E 980.2.555 |
| PROVENANCE | ex Thibault de Chambure |
| SOURCES | Collection on-line catalogue: Lander |

A simple, plain outline. See notes on recorders N5 and A2.

The foot joint is missing.

|  | A 7 |
|---|---|
| ORIGIN | Europe ?France |
| LOCATION | F – Paris : Musée de la Musique |
| COLLECTION NUMBER | E 980.2.556 |
| TYPE | Alto |
| LENGTH | c450 mm |
| PROVENANCE | ex Thibault de Chambure |
| SOURCES | Collection on-line catalogue: Lander |

A simple, plain outline. See notes on recorders N 5 and A 2.

|  | A 8 |
|---|---|
| ORIGIN | Europe ?France |
| LOCATION | F – Paris : Musée de la Musique |
| COLLECTION NUMBER | E 980.2.557 |
| TYPE | Soprano |
| LENGTH | c350 mm |
| PROVENANCE | ex Thibault de Chambure |
| SOURCES | Collection on-line catalogue: Lander |

Baroque pattern

|  | A 9 |
|---|---|
| ORIGIN | Europe ? France |
| LOCATION | F – Paris: Musée de la Musique |
| COLLECTION NUMBER | E 980.2.558 |
| MATERIALS/MOUNTS | Ivory beak and upper ring |
| PROVENANCE | ex Thibault de Chambure |
| SOURCES | Collection on-line catalogue: Lander |

The foot-joint is missing.

## A 10

| | |
|---|---|
| ORIGIN | Europe ?France |
| LOCATION | F – Paris: Musée de la Musique |
| COLLECTION NUMBER | E 2393 |
| TYPE | Mezzo soprano |
| LENGTH | 390 mm |
| MATERIALS/MOUNTS | Stained box |
| PROVENANCE | ex Cesbron |
| SOURCE | Collection on-line catalogue |

The term 'mezzo soprano' is not in common use in relation to the recorder, and at 390 mm the instrument is too small to be an alto in f' and too large to be a soprano in c"; it could be either a third or fourth flute. The lowest note is not known.

The recorder appears in Cesbron's catalogue of 1906, and was acquired by the museum in 1934.

## A 11

| | |
|---|---|
| ORIGIN | Europe ?France |
| LOCATION | F – Paris: Musée de la Musique |
| MUSEUM NUMBER | E 980.2.88 |
| TYPE | Tenor |
| LENGTH | 655 mm |
| MATERIALS/MOUNTS | Fruitwood |
| KEYS | 1 |
| MARK | A S M |
| PROVENANCE | ex Thibault de Chambure |
| SOURCE | Collection on-line catalogue |

The mark is not identified.

## A 12

| | |
|---|---|
| ORIGIN | Europe ? France |
| LOCATION | F – Paris: Musée de la musique |
| MUSEUM NUMBER | E 0355 |
| TYPE | Tenor (fourth flute) |
| LOWEST NOTE | b |

*Inventory of Recorders*

| | |
|---|---|
| LENGTH | 700 mm |
| MATERIALS/MOUNTS | Stained maple: varnished |
| SOURCE | Collection on-line catalogue |

The use of the term 'tenor' in connection with this recorder is dubious, for a tenor recorder is pitched in c'. Some authorities apply the term 'fourth flute' to recorders in b flat as well as to recorders pitched an octave higher in b flat'.

### A 13

| | |
|---|---|
| ORIGIN | La Couture-Boussey (F) |
| DATES | 1888-1896 |
| LOCATION | F – La Couture : Musée |
| COLLECTION NUMBER | 1 |
| TYPE | 'Piccolo' |
| LOWEST NOTE | c''' |
| MATERIALS/MOUNTS | Box |
| SOURCES | Lander: collection inventory |

Lander describes this instrument as a Garklein (Flötlein) a term used to describe the very small renaissance recorders in c''', but the museum inventory lists it as 'piccolo'. A number of instruments (recorders and other woodwinds) were made in La Couture-Boussey in the late nineteenth century to illustrate the history of woodwind instrument-making, many of these instruments not being playable but intended for display only (*'reconstitutions'*). In addition to the current inventory, this and the following six La Couture recorders are listed in the museum inventory of 1898, a photocopy of which was supplied to the author by Dr. Florence Gétreau (Inventaire des Instruments du Musée Communale de La Couture-Boussey, 31st. December 1898).

### A 14

| | |
|---|---|
| ORIGIN | La Couture-Boussey |
| DATES | 1888-1896 |
| LOCATION | F – La Couture: Musée |
| COLLECTION NUMBER | 2 |
| TYPE | Soprano |
| LOWEST NOTE | c'' |
| LENGTH | 310 mm |
| MATERIALS/MOUNTS | Box |
| MARK | RAFI |
| SOURCES | Gétreau (personal communication 2003): |

## collection inventory

This recorder is a nineteenth century copy of an instrument by Rafi, a family of woodwind instrument makers who flourished in Lyon in the sixteenth and seventeenth centuries. Several marks were used by the Rafi family, but all contained symbols in addition to the name 'RAFI' (*New Langwill*) and the simplified mark on this recorder has other parallels in the field of late nineteenth-century reconstructions of old instruments (compare N40).

### A 15

| | |
|---|---|
| ORIGIN | La Couture–Boussey |
| DATES | 1888-1896 |
| LOCATION | F – La Couture : Musée |
| COLLECTION NUMBER | 3 |
| TYPE | Alto |
| LOWEST NOTE | f' |
| MATERIALS/MOUNTS | stained box |
| SOURCES | Gétreau (personal communication 2003): Lander: collection inventory |

A copy of an earlier instrument, described in French as a *reconstitution*: the external form of the original is replicated but not the bore.

### A 16

| | |
|---|---|
| ORIGIN | La Couture–Boussey |
| DATES | 1888-1896 |
| LOCATION | F – La Couture : Musée |
| COLLECTION NUMBER | 5 |
| TYPE | Tenor |
| LOWEST NOTE | c' |
| LENGTH | 655 mm |
| KEYS | 1 |
| MATERIALS/MOUNTS | Box |
| SOURCES | Gétreau (personal communication 2003): Lander: collection inventory |

A *reconstitution*.

### A 17

| | |
|---|---|
| ORIGIN | La Couture-Boussey |
| DATES | 1888-1896 |
| LOCATION | F – La Couture : Musée |

*Inventory of Recorders*

| | |
|---|---|
| COLLECTION NUMBER | 6 |
| TYPE | Tenor |
| LOWEST NOTE | c' |
| KEYS | 1 |
| MARK | V/M |
| SOURCES | Gétreau (personal communication 2003): collection inventory |

This instrument is a nineteenth-century copy of a recorder by Hotteterre (the family member is not specified) and bears the mark V/M: these letters might suggest Victor (Charles) Mahillon but the instrument was made in La Couture and Mahillon did not appear to use this mark.

A 18

| | |
|---|---|
| ORIGIN | La Couture-Boussey |
| DATES | 1888-1896 |
| LOCATION | F – La Couture : Musée |
| COLLECTION NUMBER | 7 |
| TYPE | Basset |
| LOWEST NOTE | f |
| LENGTH | 910 mm |
| KEYS | 1 |
| MARK | I C DENNER |
| SOURCES | Gétreau (personal communication 2003): collection inventory |

A nineteenth-century copy of a recorder by I.C.Denner (fl c1678 – mid C18): the mark is not authentic for none of the marks used by this family consist only of the name I C DENNER (see *New Langwill*). A parallel is drawn between this mark and the mark on recorder A14.

A 19

| | |
|---|---|
| ORIGIN | La Couture-Boussey |
| DATES | 1888-1896 |
| LOCATION | F – La Couture : Musée |
| COLLECTION NUMBER | 8 |
| TYPE | Basset |
| LOWEST NOTE | f |
| LENGTH | 1050 mm |

*The Recorder In The Nineteenth Century*

| | |
|---|---|
| MATERIALS/MOUNTS | 'Light wood' |
| KEYS | 1 |
| SOURCES | Gétreau (personal communication 2003): Lander: collection inventory |

A *reconstitution*: Gétreau suggests that it is a nineteenth-century copy of a previous instrument.

### A 20

| | |
|---|---|
| ORIGIN | La Couture-Boussey |
| DATES | 1888-1896 |
| LOCATION | F – La Couture : Musée |
| COLLECTION NUMBER | 17 |
| TYPE | Alto |
| LOWEST NOTE | f' |
| LENGTH | 475 mm |
| MARK | C.F. |
| SOURCES | Gétreau (personal communication 2003): collection inventory |

A *reconstitution* which is in poor condition. The mark has not been identified.

### A 21

| | |
|---|---|
| ORIGIN | Unknown |
| LOCATION | F – Marseille: Musée Grobet-Labadié |
| COLLECTION NUMBER | 1060 |
| TYPE | Alto |
| LENGTH | 454 mm |
| MATERIALS/MOUNTS | 'light wood': foot and 'beak' in ebony: 2 horn rings |
| SOURCE | Gétreau (personal communication 2003) |

The instrument is preserved in good condition.

### A 22

| | |
|---|---|
| ORIGIN | Unknown: 1800 – 1900 |
| LOCATION | F – Marseille: Musée Grobet-Labadié |
| COLLECTION NUMBER | 1085 |
| TYPE | Alto |
| LOWEST NOTE | f' |

| | |
|---|---|
| LENGTH | 460 mm |
| MATERIALS/MOUNTS | Maple: ivory rings |
| MARK | Poorly-visible oval mark on head-joint |
| SOURCE | Gétreau (personal communication 2003) |

The instrument is described as 'dirty'.

## A 23

| | |
|---|---|
| ORIGIN | Unknown: ?1800 – 1830 |
| LOCATION | F – Nice: Musée Masséna |
| COLLECTION NUMBER | C.169 |
| TYPE | Tenor |
| LOWEST NOTE | c' |
| LENGTH | 645 mm |
| MATERIALS/MOUNTS | Maple |
| SOURCE | Gétreau (personal communication 2003) |

An instrument of mediocre manufacture and in poor condition.

## A 24

| | |
|---|---|
| ORIGIN | ? Berchtesgaden (D) |
| LOCATION | DK – Copenhagen: Musikhistorisk Museum |
| COLLECTION NUMBER | E 32 |
| TYPE | Soprano |
| LOWEST NOTE | b flat' |
| LENGTH | 373 mm |
| MATERIALS/MOUNTS | Plum unmounted |
| MAKER'S MARK | B (pitch mark) |
| SOURCES | Collection catalogue: collection catalogue (1902) : Bergstrøm (personal communications 2001, 2002) |

The museum literature suggests that this recorder is of eighteenth-century origin. However, the present author observed that the instrument bore a marked external similarity to a recorder by Lorenz Walch in the Dayton C. Miller flute collection (N59) and was also similar to several other nineteenth-century fifth and sixth flutes from Berchtesgaden which he had examined. Many of the Berchtesgaden (and other Bavarian/Austrian) recorders bear a pitch mark and in the case of the recorder under discussion the letter 'B' is clearly visible on the head-joint. 'B' is the German equivalent of the English B flat, and the length of the instrument is certainly compatible with its being a fourth flute (sixth flutes of the Berchtesgaden school are approximately 300 mm long, and the fifth flutes approximately 335 mm): it seems probable that this recorder is in fact a Berchtesgadner Fleitl in b flat'. It should also be noted that plum was often used in Berchtesgaden for recorder making. Ture Bergstrøm, curator of the collection and an authoritative maker of recorders, concurs with these observations and now lists the instrument as an anonymous recorder in b flat' of the Berchtesgaden nineteenth-century tradition.

|  | A 25 |
|---|---|
| ORIGIN | Germany |
| LOCATION | DK – Copenhagen: Musikhistorisk Museum |
| COLLECTION NUMBER | E 64 |
| TYPE | Soprano |
| LENGTH | 370 mm |
| MATERIALS/MOUNTS | Grenadilla: German silver rings and bell-rim |
| SOURCES | Collection catalogue: collection catalogue (1902) |

This recorder, together with the following two instruments, was acquired by the museum in 1900, when all three were listed as 'modern *Langsflöten*', the German term *Langsflöte* implying a vertically-blown flute. This term does not appear in other languages and it is likely that these three recorders are of nineteenth-century German origin. E64 is a keyless instrument with a clarinet-like bell and bears a superficial similarity to a 'csakan' described in Zimmermann of Leipzig's catalogue of c1900. It should be noted that the instruments in Zimmermann's catalogue are not traditional Viennese csakans as described in Chapter I.

|  | A 26 |
|---|---|
| ORIGIN | Germany |
| LOCATION | DK – Copenhagen: Musikhistorisk Museum |
| COLLECTION NUMBER | E65 |
| TYPE | Alto |
| LENGTH | 406 mm |
| MATERIALS/MOUNTS | Grenadilla: German silver rings and bell-rim |
| KEYS | 6: German silver |
| SOURCES | Collection catalogue: collection catalogue (1902) |

This keyed recorder has a clarinet-like bell. The keys and bell might suggest that the instrument is a csakan but the thumb-hole measures 5 mm in diameter, a characteristic of the recorder rather than the csakan.

## A 27

| | |
|---|---|
| ORIGIN | Germany |
| LOCATION | DK – Copenhagen: Musikhistorisk Museum |
| COLLECTION NUMBER | E 66 |
| TYPE | Alto |
| LENGTH | 343 mm |
| MATERIALS/MOUNTS | Grenadilla: German silver rings and bell-rim: 2 pieces |
| KEYS | 6: German silver |
| SOURCES | Collection catalogue: collection catalogue (1902) |

The instrument has a straight, unflared foot-joint and the keywork bears a similarity to the previous recorder (A26, collection number E65). The thumb-hole measures 4.7 mm (recorder size) but with a length of only 343 mm the recorder is a soprano rather than an alto as described in the museum literature.

## A 28

| | |
|---|---|
| ORIGIN | Unknown: c1900 |
| LOCATION | NL – The Hague: Gemeentemuseum |
| COLLECTION NUMBER | 1933 0686 |
| TYPE | Soprano |
| LENGTH | 362 mm |
| MATERIALS/MOUNTS | 1 piece |
| SOURCE | Collection inventory |

## A 29

| | |
|---|---|
| ORIGIN | Unknown: c1875 |
| LOCATION | NL – The Hague: Gemeentemuseum |
| COLLECTION NUMBER | 1933 1008 |
| TYPE | Sopranino |
| LENGTH | 224 mm |
| MATERIALS/MOUNTS | Fruitwood: 1 piece |
| SOURCE | Collection inventory |

## A 30

| | |
|---|---|
| ORIGIN | Unknown: c1850 |
| LOCATION | NL – The Hague: Gemeentemuseum |
| MUSEUM NUMBER | 1933 1041 |
| TYPE | Alto |

| | |
|---|---|
| LENGTH | 514 mm |
| MATERIALS/MOUNTS | Box: horn rings |
| KEYS | 3: brass |
| SOURCE | Collection inventory |

The instrument measures 514 mm and is long for an alto but the pitch of the lowest note is not known. Three keys on an instrument of this size is an unusual feature.

### A 31

| | |
|---|---|
| ORIGIN | ? Nuremberg: a1860 |
| LOCATION | D – Nuremberg: Germanisches Nationalmuseum |
| COLLECTION NUMBER | MI 93 |
| TYPE | Bass |
| SOURCES | Collection on-line inventory: Lander |

The museum inventory describes the recorder as a 'theatre instrument', and Lander refers to it as a 'stage prop'. The present author has not yet been able to examine this instrument.

### A 32

| | |
|---|---|
| ORIGIN | ? Austria: c1900 |
| LOCATION | A – Graz – S: Stadtmuseum |
| COLLECTION NUMBER | SM 1 |
| TYPE | Sixth flute |
| LOWEST NOTE | d" |
| LENGTH | 285 mm |
| MATERIALS/MOUNTS | Grenadilla |
| SOURCE | Collection catalogue |

Described as 'without beak': in this respect it bears a similarity to N52, also made in Graz but in the workshop of Heinrich Schweffer.

### A 33

| | |
|---|---|
| ORIGIN | ?Germany ??Scandinavia |
| LOCATION | GB – London: Horniman Museum |
| COLLECTION NUMBER | 14.5.47/59 |
| TYPE | Third flute |
| LOWEST NOTE | a' |
| LENGTH | 391 mm |

| | |
|---|---|
| MATERIALS/MOUNTS | Plum: foot is of ?box |
| PROVENANCE | ex Carse |
| SOURCES | Lander: Strauchen (personal communication 2002) |

Carse described the instrument as being of brown wood (?laburnum) with a bell in a lighter wood which appeared to be a replacement. He listed the instrument as "France ?18th century".

Friedrich von Huene examined the recorder in 1988 and noted that the foot-joint was not original: he considered the instrument to be rather crude and suggested that it was of German or Scandinavian nineteenth-century origin. There was little activity in the field of the recorder in Scandinavia until the 1930s so the origin of the recorder is more likely to be German - assuming that von Huene's conjecture is correct.

## A 34

| | |
|---|---|
| ORIGIN | Tunisia |
| LOCATION | B – Brussels: Musée des Instruments de Musique |
| COLLECTION NUMBER | M 359 |
| TYPE | Alto |
| LENGTH | 530 mm |
| MATERIALS/MOUNTS | Blackwood: ivory rings |
| SOURCES | De Keyser (personal communication 2003): Mahillon I: museum visit |

This instrument is of simple shape and bears a superficial resemblance to the Colas alto N5, the Noblet recorder (N45) and the anonymous French recorders A2, A6, A7, and A35. It is longer than the other altos of this appearance. Tunisia was a French Protectorate from 1881 to 1956, so the similarity to the French instruments is explicable; however, it is open to speculation as to whether the recorder was made in Tunisia or was acquired from a Frenchman living in the protectorate. The recorder came into Mahillon's possession in 1877 and was exhibited in Paris the following year.

## A 35

| | |
|---|---|
| ORIGIN | Unknown ?France |
| LOCATION | US – MI – Ann Arbor: Stearns Collection |
| COLLECTION NUMBER | 504 |
| TYPE | Alto |
| LOWEST NOTE | f' |
| LENGTH | 468 mm |
| MATERIALS/MOUNTS | Box: horn ferrules |

*The Recorder In The Nineteenth Century*

SOURCES                             Collection catalogue: Warner and von Huene (1970)

The instrument exhibits the same simple outline as the recorder by Colas (N5) in the same collection, and also recorders N45, A2, A6, A7 and A34, the shape suggesting a similar French origin. It is not in playing condition. See notes on A2.

|  | A 36 |
|---|---|
| ORIGIN | ?England ?Germany |
| LOCATION | US – NY – New York: Metropolitan Museum of art |
| COLLECTION NUMBER | 89.4.1511 |
| TYPE | Alto |
| LENGTH | 475 mm |
| LOWEST NOTE | f' |
| MATERIALS/MOUNTS | Box: horn ferrules and beak |
| PROVENANCE | Crosby Brown Collection |
| SOURCES | Lander: collection catalogue: collection catalogue 1902[31] |

There are some discrepancies between the 1902 catalogue of the Crosby Brown Collection and the current catalogue concerning a number of the recorders in the Metropolitan Museum of Art, New York. In the 1902 catalogue the recorders are referred to as *Flûtes douces* whereas in the current catalogue they are listed as recorders, although this is a matter of terminology rather than organological significance.

The 1902 catalogue suggests that this recorder may be of German origin but the current catalogue describes it as English.

|  | A 37 |
|---|---|
| ORIGIN | ?Scandinavia |
| LOCATION | US – NY – New York: Metropolitan Museum of Art |
| COLLECTION NUMBER | 89.4.2646 |
| TYPE | Alto |
| LENGTH | 445 mm |
| MATERIALS/MOUNTS | Mahogany head and body: fruitwood foot: antler or horn rings: antler or bone lip plate and antler inlaid dots on head |
| PROVENANCE | Crosby Brown Collection |
| SOURCES | Lander: collection catalogue |

---

[31] Catalogue of the Crosby Brown Collection of Musical Instruments, (New York: Metropolitan Museum of Art 1902-1905)

*Inventory of Recorders*

This recorder is not listed in the 1902 catalogue but is currently described as ex Crosby Brown. A Scandinavian origin is unlikely as no recorder activity is described in that region before c1930.

                              A 38

| | |
|---|---|
| MAKER | Unknown ?KYNSEKER, H.F. or MAHILLON, V-C. |
| PLACE OF WORK | Unknown ?Nuremberg (D) or Brussels (B) |
| DATES | 1636 – 1686 (H.F.K.): 1841 – 1924 (V-C.M.) |
| LOCATION | US – NY –New York: Metropolitan Museum of Art |
| COLLECTION NUMBER | 89.4.2695 |
| TYPE | Soprano |
| LOWEST NOTE | c" or c sharp" ('high c' in 1902 catalogue) |
| LENGTH | 318 mm |
| MATERIALS/MOUNTS | Plum: horn mounts: 2 pieces |
| MARK | HEIRONYMUS [and] H F |
| PROVENANCE | Crosby Brown Collection |
| SOURCES | Lander: collection catalogue: collection catalogue 1902 |

Controversy surrounds both this and the following two instruments, there being debate regarding the maker and (consequently the date) of the recorders. All are of the renaissance type. Lander ascribes the recorders to Mahillon, who is known to have made copies of renaissance recorders including copies of the Kynseker instruments in the Germanisches Nationalmuseum in Nuremberg (N31 – 38 in the present series). In 1974 Libin noted in the collection records that x-ray examination suggested that the instruments were indeed similar to the Nuremberg set and ascribed the recorders to Kynseker rather than to an anonymous nineteenth-century maker. In 1976 van der Meer, then curator of the Nuremberg collection, thought that the instruments may be Kynsekers but questioned both the flat windway over the block and also the maker's mark which did not precisely match that on the Nuremberg recorders. A year later von Huene considered the three recorders to be original and authentic, commenting that "no copies of this quality are known to have been made in the nineteenth or early twentieth centuries". In 1978 Hellwig examined the recorders and considered them not to be authentic because of the finish, the light weight, and the style of lettering on the stamp.

The evidence that these recorders date from the seventeenth century is far from compelling in view of the inconsistencies noted by van der Meer and Hellwig. In the light of von Huene's comments, it should be noted that Mahillon's Kynseker copies (N31 – 38) are well made and were used in public performance. The inconsistency in the maker's mark is of note, for other nineteenth-century reproductions often bear inconsistent marks (note particularly recorder N40, a copy by Mahillon of a recorder by Rauch which is unauthentically stamped).

The pitch of the recorders is unusual: the pitch standard to which they are compared is not known, so they may represent low-pitched recorders in d", g' and d', a system compatible with the renaissance consort.

This recorder, together with the following two, could well be part of a consort but the appropriate bass recorder has not come to light.

In conclusion, the present author is of the opinion that these renaissance-style recorders are most probably of nineteenth-century manufacture, this opinion being confirmed by the 1902 catalogue which lists the instruments as reproductions.

### A 39

| | |
|---|---|
| ORIGIN | Unknown ?KYNSEKER or MAHILLON |
| LOCATION | US – NY – New York: Metropolitan Museum of Art |
| COLLECTION NUMBER | 89.4.2663 |
| TYPE | Alto |
| LOWEST NOTE | f sharp' ('G' in 1902 catalogue) |
| LENGTH | 449 mm |
| MATERIALS/MOUNTS | Plum: horn mounts |
| PROVENANCE | Crosby Brown Collection |
| SOURCES | Lander: collection catalogue: collection catalogue 1902 |

An alto, otherwise similar to A 38.

### A 40

| | |
|---|---|
| ORIGIN | Unknown ?KYNSEKER or MAHILLON |
| LOCATION | US – NY – New York: Metropolitan Museum of Art |
| COLLECTION NUMBER | 89.4.2644 |
| TYPE | Tenor |
| LOWEST NOTE | c sharp' ('alto in C' in 1902 catalogue) |
| LENGTH | 591 mm |
| MATERIALS/MOUNTS | Plum: horn mounts |
| PROVENANCE | Crosby Brown Collection |
| SOURCES | Lander: collection catalogue: collection catalogue 1902 |

A tenor, otherwise similar to A 38/39.

*Inventory of Recorders*

## A 41

| | |
|---|---|
| ORIGIN | Unknown: nineteenth century |
| LOCATION | US – NY – New York: Metropolitan Museum of Art |
| COLLECTION NUMBER | 89.4.2926 |
| TYPE | Tenor |
| LOWEST NOTE | b |
| LENGTH | 697 mm |
| MATERIALS/MOUNTS | Stained maple: brass rings |
| KEYS | 1: brass |
| PROVENANCE | Crosby Brown Collection |
| SOURCES | Lander: collection catalogue |

A renaissance-style instrument with fontanelle, probably of European origin.

## A 42

| | |
|---|---|
| ORIGIN | Unknown: nineteenth century |
| LOCATION | US – NY – New York: Metropolitan Museum of Art |
| COLLECTION NUMBER | 89.4.2045 |
| TYPE | Basset |
| LOWEST NOTE | g |
| LENGTH | 938 mm |
| MATERIALS/MOUNTS | Stained box: brass rings |
| KEYS | 1: brass |
| PROVENANCE | Crosby Brown Collection |
| SOURCES | Lander: collection catalogue: 1902 collection catalogue |

A renaissance-style basset recorder with fontanelle. The 1902 catalogue describes it as a reproduction obtained by courtesy of Frederico Vellani, then director of the Museo Liceo Musicale in Bologna.

## A 43

| | |
|---|---|
| ORIGIN | Unknown: nineteenth century |
| LOCATION | US – NY – New York: Metropolitan Museum of Art |
| COLLECTION NUMBER | 89.4.682 |
| TYPE | Contrabass |
| LOWEST NOTE | D |
| LENGTH | 2602 mm |
| MATERIALS/MOUNTS | Stained maple: brass rings |

| | |
|---|---|
| KEYS | 4: brass |
| MARK | Trefoil |
| PROVENANCE | ex Galpin: Crosby Brown Collection |
| SOURCES | Lander: collection catalogue: 1902 collection catalogue |

    This instrument is described as "Reproduction. Original in Le Musée d'antiquities du Steen, Antwerp: after Hans Rauch von Schratt". It is in the renaissance style with fontanelle and blown with a crook, the 1902 catalogue describing it as a reproduction of a sixteenth-century instrument by courtesy of Baron de Vinck de Winnezeale, then director of the museum. It was at one time in Galpin's possession.

    A further copy of the Antwerp instrument by Mahillon is listed as N41 but this instrument is some 18 mm longer than the present one. For further details, see recorder N41. The mark is not consistent with Rauch, an inconsistency previously noted in other nineteenth-century reproductions (see N40, A14, A18, A38 - 40).

### A 44

| | |
|---|---|
| ORIGIN | ?France: C19 |
| LOCATION | US – NY – New York: Metropolitan Museum of Art |
| COLLECTION NUMBER | 89.4.2352 |
| TYPE | Contrabass (great bass) |
| LENGTH | 1505 mm |
| LOWEST NOTE | ?d ??D |
| MATERIALS/MOUNTS | Stained maple: brass mounts |
| KEYS | 3: brass |
| PROVENANCE | Crosby Brown Collection |
| SOURCES | Lander: collection catalogue: 1902 collection catalogue |

    A renaissance-style recorder with fontanelle and blown through a crook. The catalogue describes the instrument as a great bass in D whereas Lander calls it a contrabass (these differences are of little significance). A fundamental of D would be appropriate for a great bass/contrabass but the length of the recorder would suggest that this note is more likely to be d. Although listed with other reproductions in the 1902 catalogue, neither this nor the current catalogue describes the recorder as a reproduction but no other French bass recorders of nineteenth-century origin have come to light in the course of the present study.

*Inventory of Recorders*

|  |  |
|---|---|
|  | A 45 |
| ORIGIN | Unknown |
| LOCATION | US – DC – Washington – Smithsonian |
| COLLECTION NUMBER | 65.0615 |
| TYPE | Soprano |
| LOWEST NOTE | c" |
| LENGTH | 360 mm |
| MATERIALS/MOUNTS | ?box ?plum ?maple: unmounted |
| PROVENANCE | ex University of Pennsylvania |
| SOURCES | Collection catalogue: Sheldon (personal communication 1981) |

The museum catalogue comments that the instrument may be "the work of an amateur or folk craftsman". The recorder is in the baroque style.

|  |  |
|---|---|
|  | A46 |
| ORIGIN | Unknown |
| DATES | c1840 |
| LOCATION | ex Coleman ? USA – CA - Claremont – Fiske |
| TYPE | 6th flute |
| MATERIALS/MOUNTS | Box |
| KEYS | 1 |
| MAKER'S MARK | D (pitch mark) |
| SOURCE | Rice (personal communication 2007) |

|  |  |
|---|---|
|  | A47 |
| ORIGIN | ? English |
| DATES | 1890-1910 |
| LOCATION | Australia – Sydney: Powerhouse Museum |
| COLLECTION NUMBER | H4826 |
| TYPE | ?Alto |
| MATERIALS/MOUNTS | Box: silver rings |
| SOURCE | Lander (personal communication, also database) |

Thought to be of English origin: plain outline with offset finger-holes

|  |  |
|---|---|
|  | E 1 |
| MAKER | GRASSI, Barnaba |
| DATES | fl a1797 – p1802 |

| | |
|---|---|
| PLACE OF WORK | Milan (I) |
| LOCATION | I – Rome: Museo degli Strumenti Musicali |
| COLLECTION NUMBER | 638 |
| TYPE | Alto |
| MATERIALS/MOUNTS | Box: ivory mounts |
| SOURCES | Collection on-line catalogue: Lander: *New Langwill*: Young |

The family of Grassi is documented as being active in Milan as instrument makers and dealers during the dates given above: Barnaba Grassi and his son Antonio were the active members of the family, and both *New Langwill* and Young ascribe this recorder to Barnaba. Lander (2007) lists two instruments in this collection by Grassi: one is illustrated in the collection catalogue and fits the description of a recorder in three pieces with two rings in ivory and one in metal. The Accession Number is given as 881.

### E 2

| | |
|---|---|
| MAKER | GRASSI, Barnaba |
| LOCATION | D – Leipzig: Universität |
| COLLECTION NUMBER | 1113 |
| TYPE | Exilent |
| LOWEST NOTE | g" |
| LENGTH | 251 mm |
| MATERIALS/MOUNTS | Box: horn rings |
| MARK | GRASSI/ IN MILAN [the 'ns' are reversed] |
| SOURCES | Lander: collection catalogue: *New Langwill*: Young |

Heyde, writing in the museum catalogue, gives Barnaba and Antonio Grassi as makers. The recorder is in the form of a baroque instrument. 'Exilent' is a term sometimes applied to recorders smaller than the sopranino in f" such as the renaissance Garklein Flötlein in c'".

### E 3

| | |
|---|---|
| MAKER | GRENSER, Heinrich |
| DATES | fl1796 – 1813 |
| PLACE OF WORK | Dresden (D) |
| LOCATION | xD – Berlin: Institut für Musikforschung |
| COLLECTION NUMBER | x2810 |
| TYPE | Alto |
| LENGTH | 570 mm |

| | |
|---|---|
| MATERIALS/MOUNTS | Box: ivory mounts |
| KEYS | 3: brass |
| MARK | (crown)/ H.GRENSER/ DRESDEN |
| PROVENANCE | ex Sachs |
| SOURCES | Lander: *New Langwill*: Young |

   This recorder had a clarinet-like bell and keys for d', e', and f sharp'. Lander suggests that it may be a csakan because of its keys and bell but the instrument was made in Dresden not Vienna and the keywork is not typical of that found on csakans. It is in an unusual pitch for a recorder and it is possible that it could represent a high-pitched recorder in e flat', a type occasionally found amongst recorders of the baroque period.

   Heinrich Grenser, a member of the Grenser dynasty of instrument makers, was a prolific maker of woodwind instruments but this is the only recorder known to have been made by him. Sadly it is now lost.

### E 4

| | |
|---|---|
| MAKER | WALCH, Lorenz I |
| DATES | 1735 – 1809 |
| PLACE OF WORK | Berchtesgaden (D) |
| LOCATION | A – Salzburg: Museo Carolino Augusteum |
| MUSEUM NUMBER | 3/4 |
| TYPE | Alto |
| LOWEST NOTE | g' |
| LENGTH | 420 mm |
| MATERIALS/MOUNTS | Plum: horn mounts |
| MARK | L.WALCH [in scroll]/ (shell) |
| SOURCES | Museum visit: *New Langwill*: Young |

   Lorenz Walch I was the father of Lorenz II and grandfather of Paul, whose recorders are listed as N57 – 68. The Walch family of Berchtesgaden is discussed in Chapter V, 'The Berchtesgadner Fleitl'.

### E 5

| | |
|---|---|
| MAKER | WALCH, Lorenz I |
| LOCATION | D – Bavaria: secret private collection |
| TYPE | Alto |
| LOWEST NOTE | f' |
| LENGTH | 508 mm |
| MATERIALS/MOUNTS | Plum: unmounted |

*The Recorder In The Nineteenth Century*

SOURCES                      Young: Young[32]

Young (1982) notes that this instrument was in the possession of an old Nuremberg family until c1850 and used for amateur music-making. It then passed into the hands of the Bogenhauser Künstlerkapelle (see Chapter IX, 'The Revival of the Recorder'). Young was taken to a secret location in Bavaria to study this and other instruments.

E 6

| | |
|---|---|
| MAKER | WALCH, Lorenz I |
| LOCATION | D – Berchtesgaden: Heimatmuseum |
| COLLECTION NUMBER | 1071 |
| TYPE | 'Sopranino' |
| LOWEST NOTE | e flat" |
| LENGTH | 269 mm |
| MATERIALS/MOUNTS | Plum: unmounted: 2 pieces |
| MARK | L:WALCH |
| SOURCES | Bruckner (1978): museum visit |

E flat is an unusual key for a sopranino.

E 7

| | |
|---|---|
| MAKER | WALCH, Lorenz I |
| LOCATION | D – Berchtesgaden: Heimatmuseum |
| COLLECTION NUMBER | 1072 |
| TYPE | Sixth flute |
| LOWEST NOTE | d" |
| LENGTH | 301 mm |
| MATERIALS/MOUNTS | Plum: unmounted: 2 pieces |
| SOURCES | Bruckner (1978): museum visit |

E 8

| | |
|---|---|
| ORIGIN | Anonymous: circa C19 |
| LOCATION | US – DC – Washington: DCM |
| COLLECTION NUMBER | 0835 |
| TYPE | Alto |
| LOWEST NOTE | f' |
| LENGTH | 482 mm |
| MATERIALS/MOUNTS | Box |
| SOURCE | Collection on-line catalogue: Ward-Bamford |

---

32    Young, P.T. 'Some further Instruments by the Denners', *Galpin Society Journal* XXXV (1982), pp78-85

(personal communication 2002)

Correspondence from the museum suggests that, whereas there is a possibility that this instrument may be of eighteenth-century origin, it is more likely to date from the nineteenth century. It is described as "not a sophisticated instrument".

### E 9

| | |
|---|---|
| ORIGIN | Unknown: France c1790 – 1815 |
| LOCATION | CH – Reinach: Tarasov (private collection) |
| TYPE | Fourth flute |
| LOWEST NOTE | b flat' |
| MATERIALS/MOUNTS | Box |
| SOURCE | Tarasov (personal communication 2003) |

An anonymous recorder from a French estate: it has a chromatic compass of more than two octaves.

### D 1

| | |
|---|---|
| MAKER | BAINBRIDGE, William |
| DATES | fl1809 – 1834 |
| PLACE OF WORK | London (GB) |
| LOCATION | Unknown |
| SOURCE | Catalogue of the International Inventions Exhibition London 1885 |

This catalogue is the sole reference to this recorder and its present location is unknown. No other recorders by this maker have been discovered, Bainbridge being chiefly known as a maker and developer of the flageolet: he played the flute, oboe, and flageolet, inventing double and triple versions of that instrument. Many of these are extant.

### D 2

| | |
|---|---|
| MAKER | BERTANI, Domenico (perhaps modifier) |
| DATES | late C18/ early C19 |
| PLACE OF WORK | Modena (I) |
| LOCATION | I – Modena |
| COLLECTION NUMBER | 23 |
| LENGTH | 670 mm |
| MATERIALS/MOUNTS | Maple: 4 pieces |
| KEYS | 1: brass |

| | |
|---|---|
| MARK | D.Bertani. Modena |
| SOURCE | Museum catalogue |

Described as *Flauto dolce, gia* (formerly) *flauto d'amore con una chiave* (with one key), it has been irrationally modified to falsify its nature and appearance. The head joint has been turned into that of a recorder and a hole for the little finger has been bored. Apart from the key, it otherwise bears a superficial likeness to the four-jointed tenor recorders of Thomas Stanesby, jr.

Bertani was, in the words of *New Langwill*, a bad string instrument maker who also made woodwind instruments. A few other woodwind instruments survive.

I am indebted to Renato Meucci for drawing my attention to this instrument.

## D 3

| | |
|---|---|
| MAKER | BOIE, Johann Friedrich |
| DATES | 1762 – 1809 |
| PLACE OF WORK | Göttingen (D) |
| LOCATION | N – Trondheim: Ringve |
| COLLECTION NUMBER | RMT 78/6 |
| TYPE | Alto |
| LOWEST NOTE | f' |
| LENGTH | 343 mm |
| MATERIALS/MOUNTS | Ebony: ivory rings and bell-rim |
| KEYS | 2: silver |
| SOURCES | Birley (personal communication 1981): Lander: Krouthen (personal communication 2004) |

In 1983 MacMillan (using information supplied by Birley) described this instrument as a treble recorder in blackwood from an unknown private collection.[33] Lander currently describes it as a recorder with a flageolet head.

The recorder is now at Trondheim and the following information was obtained from the curator, Mats Krouthen. It is described as a recorder of ebony in six pieces with a flageolet head and in three pieces. There is a flageolet mouthpiece with five channels leading to a sponge chamber. The flageolet head can be put onto the recorder mouthpiece but the instrument can also be played as a recorder (three pieces). There is a key on the foot for the fourth finger of the left hand and a covered key on the mouthpiece to facilitate high trills. This key is a feature of the flageolet rather than of the recorder. When played as a recorder the tone is bright in the upper register, but somewhat softer when played as a flageolet.

F is an unusual key for the flageolet.

---

33   MacMillan, D., 'The Recorder in the late eighteenth and early nineteenth Centuries' pp489-497

## D 4

| | |
|---|---|
| MAKER | DESTUYVER, J.B |
| DATES | fl lateC19/ early C20 |
| PLACE OF WORK | Ghent (B) |
| LOCATION | B – Brussels |
| COLLECTION NUMBER | M 2650 |
| TYPE | Alto |
| LOWEST NOTE | f' |
| MATERIALS/MOUNTS | Stained ?box: horn rings and beak |
| MARK | J.B.Destuyver à Gand |
| SOURCES | Mahillon IV: museum visit |

This instrument may be of early twentieth-century origin: no other woodwind instruments by Destuyver are known. The recorder is listed in Mahillon's catalogue of 1912, where it is described as *Taille de flûte douce,* a term which is translated as tenor recorder. The pitch, however, is consistent with an alto. The biographical details are taken from *New Langwill*.

## D 5

| | |
|---|---|
| MAKER | FIRTH, POND, & Co. |
| DATES | 1856 – 1862 |
| PLACE OF WORK | New York (US) |
| LOCATION | Unknown |
| TYPE | 'The size of an alto' |
| KEYS | 1 |
| MARK | FIRTH, POND, and Co./ BROADWAY/ NEW YORK |
| PROVENANCE | Sold by G. King in 1963 |
| SOURCE | Thompson |

The instrument is the subject of an article by Thompson published in 1961.[34] It is approximately the size of an alto recorder but has a sponge chamber with a centre blowing hole and a closed key below the lowest tone hole (a similar chamber is found on two other recorders in the present series, N15 and D3). The instrument is an hybrid, with features of the flageolet incorporated into a recorder-type duct flute. The touch-key is not characteristic of either instrument and no similar instruments have come to light.

---

34  Thompson, R. 'The Anachronistic Recorder',
*The American Recorder* II 4 (1961) p3

Kuronen considers the instrument to be a flageolet.[35]

As a footnote to Thompson's article, Anderson comments that "fipple flutes under the name of 'flageolets' were used in marching bands in the American Civil War" and postulates that this instrument may represent this unusual genre. The possible use of recorders in this context is discussed under 'The use of the recorder' in Chapter VI.

The firm of Firth, Pond, & Co. flourished in New York between 1847 and 1863, Firth and Pond being associated at times with Hall. The firm both made and sold instruments.

D 6

| | |
|---|---|
| MAKER | ?GALPIN, F.W. |
| LOCATION | US – MA – Boston: Museum of Fine Arts |
| COLLECTION NUMBER | 17.1738 |
| TYPE | Third flute |
| LOWEST NOTE | a' |
| LENGTH | 375 mm |
| MATERIALS/MOUNTS | Walnut |
| PROVENANCE | ex Galpin |
| SOURCES | Bessaraboff: collection on-line catalogue ; Kuronen (personal communication 2002) |

Bessaraboff (1941) considers this instrument to be of eighteenth-century origin, but Kuronen thinks it is more likely to be a nineteenth-century recorder by Galpin, particularly as it is of walnut, a timber used in other Galpin reproductions. This wood is not commonly used for recorders. The recorder is a poorly made instrument in the baroque style and emanated from Galpin's collection which was acquired by the Boston museum in 1915/16.

For further details of Galpin, see recorder N7 and Chapter IX 'The Recorder Revival'.

D 7

| | |
|---|---|
| MAKER | GOULDING D'ALMAINE & Co. |
| DATES | fl1803 – 1824 |
| PLACE OF WORK | London (GB) |
| LOCATION | Unknown |
| TYPE | Alto |
| SOURCES | Bingham (personal communication 2002): *New Langwill* |

---

35  Kuronen, D. Letter to the Editor, *American Recorder* XLV 1 (2004) p25

In a personal communication Bingham indicated that the recorder had passed through his hands but he was unsure of its present location: the instrument is listed in *New Langwill* as belonging to Bingham.

The firm of Goulding traded under several partnerships between 1786 and 1834: Thomas D'Almaine was associated with Goulding between 1803 and 1836. Between 1825 and 1836 the firm traded under the titles 'Goulding, D'Almaine & Co.' and also 'Goulding, D'Almaine'.

## D 8

| | |
|---|---|
| MAKER | LOT, Lucien |
| DATES | fl c1946 |
| PLACE OF WORK | France ?Paris |
| LOCATION | Unknown: recently sold (2003) by Initial Music |
| TYPE | Soprano |
| MATERIALS/MOUNTS | Palisander: brass mouthpiece |
| KEYS | 6: nickel silver |
| SOURCES | Initial music on-line sales catalogue:[36] Lander |

This recorder is included as an example of the confusion sometimes engendered in the organology of nineteenth- and twentieth-century 'unorthodox' recorders. The family Lot existed as instrument makers in Paris from the early eighteenth century until the middle of the twentieth century: Louis Lot (1807 – 1896) established a workshop in Paris which continued to flourish after his death, and a further L. Lot (Lucien Lot, abbreviated Ln. Lot) is reported to have worked in Paris around 1946 (*New Langwill*).

Lander attributes this instrument to L.Lot, suggesting that is of nineteenth-century origin. Cécile Robert, in her 1998 book on the rediscovery of the recorder in France, also comments on the instrument.[37] She states that the last attempts at making recorders in France lay in the hands of Louis Lot in 1873 who made (on the basis of the traditional *flûte douce*) an hybrid instrument with six keys to facilitate playing. Robert quotes Clowez' treatise of 1946, which noted that pupils enjoyed playing the six-keyed recorder and found it easier to play the difficult passages on it than on the standard recorder. Finally, she writes that it is interesting to accord to the flute of Lot 'a title of curiosity': his rapport with the instrument and its repertoire appeared distant. There is a drawing of an instrument apparently identical to the recorder under discussion.

Initial Music (a firm specializing in antiquarian instruments) advertised the recorder for sale in 2003 as being by Ln. Lot and therefore a twentieth-century instrument. The catalogue of the Sallaberry Collection (see N 24, 25) illustrates an almost identical soprano recorder

---

36   http://perso.orange.fr/initial-music/
37   Robert,C., *XXème siècle et flûte à bec: sa redécouverte en France*,
(Bourg –la- Reine: Zurfluh 1998), p79

*The Recorder In The Nineteenth Century*

with a length of 328 mm and bearing six keys. This instrument is also in palisander with nickel-silver keys but the mouthpiece tip is of ivory. The instrument bears the mark Ln/ LOT/ FRANCE/ BREVET S.G.D.G.[38] the mark given for Lucien Lot by *New Langwill*.

I conclude that the instrument (and also the one illustrated in Robert) are by Lucien Lot and of twentieth-century origin in view of the compelling similarity to the Sallaberry instruments and the information provided by that instrument's stamp. Close examination of the available (on-line) images of the recorder suggest that the brass mouthpiece is an illusion, and that the brass would have been covered by a lost ivory cap. Clowez' method of 1946 alludes to recorders by 'L.' Lot both without key and with six keys. In the present author's opinion it is unlikely that a book published in 1946 would seek to relate to an obscure curiosity made three-quarters of a century ago, and would more likely to relate to an instrument of contemporary manufacture and availability. Giannini, the definitive biographer of the Lot family, makes no mention of recorders by the nineteenth-century Louis Lot.[39]

In 1963 Glassgold published a description of a keyed recorder but which modern scholarship suggests is a csakan.[40] His interest in keyed recorders continued, for in a subsequent issue he commented that he had recently acquired a six-keyed recorder by the French manufacturer L.Lot "who recently died", the instrument being a soprano in c".[41] Since the maker is known to have "recently died" (the article was written in 1964) it seems probable that Glassgold incorrectly ascribed his recorder to Louis rather than Lucien, for his description suggests that the instrument is indeed comparable with those of Lucien Lot described above.

|  | D 9 |
| --- | --- |
| MAKE | ?MARTIN |
| DATES | ?C19 |
| PLACE OF WORK | La Couture-Boussey (F) |
| LOCATION | F – La Couture : Musée |
| COLLECTION NUMBER | 15 |
| TYPE | Soprano |
| LOWEST NOTE | c" |
| MATERIALS/MOUNTS | Box |
| SOURCE | Collection inventory |

The museum inventory ascribes this instrument to Martin, but points out that it is unstamped. A family of Martins was active in La Couture from the middle of the eighteenth

---

38 *sans garantie du gouvernment* i.e. patented but without government guarantee
39 Giannini, T., *Great Flute Makers of France: the Lot and Godefroy families 1650 – 1900*, (London: Tony Bingham 1993)
40 Glassgold, A. C. 'Another Anachronism?', *The American Recorder* III 3 (1963), p15
41 Glassgold, A.C. Letter 'More about keyed Recorders', *The American Recorder* IV 2 (1964), p27

century (Jean Baptiste, b1751/2) to the late nineteenth century (Jean-François, 1794 – 1876, active p1827): see also notes to recorder N44. Further members of the family opened a business in Paris which flourished from 1840 to 1927 (*New Langwill*). The recorder is listed in the 1898 inventory (see A13) where it is described simply as a recorder in boxwood without key.

D 10

| | |
|---|---|
| MAKER | RUDALL CARTE & Co. |
| DATES | 1872 – p1950 |
| LOCATION | GB – Oxford: Bate Collection |
| COLLECTION NUMBER | 0116 |
| TYPE | Tenor |
| LENGTH | 633 mm |
| MATERIALS/MOUNTS | 2 pieces: brass ferrule |
| MARK | Hare's ears |
| PROVENANCE | ex Hunt |
| SOURCES | Lander: collection on-line catalogue: museum visit |

This instrument is in the renaissance style in two pieces and is a copy of a recorder by Bassano (C16-C17) in the Dayton C. Miller Flute Collection in Washington D.C. The head may be rotated so that the window may face backwards or forwards.

A similar recorder is illustrated in Welch's *Six Lectures on the Recorder* (Lecture III, delivered in 1902), Welch describing the instrument as having been lent by Messrs. Rudall Carte and dating from the sixteenth or seventeenth century.[12] The recorder illustrated does not bear the stamp of Rudall Carte but the 'hare's ears' of Bassano.

A personal communication from Margaret Birley in 1981 advised that the instrument had passed through Sotheby's Sale Rooms in 1978, at which point a date of *circa* 1896 was given for it.

This recorder may date from the very late nineteenth or very early twentieth centuries, and, along with the Galpin instruments (N7-19), represents one of the earliest products of the recorder revival in England.

D 11

| | |
|---|---|
| MAKER | SATTLER (family) |
| DATES | ?C18 ?C19 |
| PLACE OF WORK | Leipzig (D) |
| LOCATION | D – Leipzig: Universität |
| COLLECTION NUMBER | 1116 |
| TYPE | Soprano |

---

42   Welch, C., *Six Lectures on the Recorder and other Flutes in relation to Literature*, p165

*The Recorder In The Nineteenth Century*

| | |
|---|---|
| LENGTH | ?375 mm |
| MATERIALS/MOUNTS | Box |
| MARK | S  A (less clearly visible) |
| SOURCE | Collection catalogue (Heyde) |

    The head of this recorder was lost in the Second World War. The middle and foot joints are stamped 'S' and, in addition, there is a less clear mark 'A' on the middle joint.

    Four generations of the Sattler family were active in Leipzig from the early eighteenth century and used the mark 'S' in the latter half of that century. The presence of the 'A' suggests either Carl Andreas Wilhelm (1738 – 1788) or possibly Friedrich August (1775 – 1850). No other recorders by the Sattlers appear to have survived.

### D 12

| | |
|---|---|
| MAKER | SMART, George |
| DATES | 1773 – 1805 (see below) |
| PLACE OF WORK | London (GB) |
| LOCATION | US – DC – Washington: DCM |
| COLLECTION NUMBER | DCM 1159 |
| TYPE | Alto |
| LOWEST NOTE | f' |
| LENGTH | 499 mm |
| MATERIALS/MOUNTS | Box |
| MARK | SMART/. |
| PROVENANCE | ex W.Howard Head |
| SOURCE | Lander: collection on-line catalogue |

    Smart was an instrument maker, music seller, and publisher who had a business in London: he was succeeded by one William Turnbull. Lander gives Smart's dates as 1773 – 1805, whereas *New Langwill* gives late eighteenth century.

### D 13

| | |
|---|---|
| MAKER | WREDE, Hermann |
| DATES | fl1810 – 1857 |
| PLACE OF WORK | London (GB) |
| LOCATION | US – NC – Duke University: Eddy |
| LENGTH | 313 mm |
| MATERIALS/MOUNTS | box: ivory studs |
| KEYS | 1 |

SOURCE                          Collection on-line catalogue: Neece (personal
                                communication 2007)

This instrument was originally a flageolet but has been turned into a recorder by carving the tenon of the duct joint into a recorder mouthpiece, or possibly a recorder with a strange mouthpiece joint (collection catalogue).

Wrede worked in London as an instrument maker, dealer, and importer. A number of other woodwind instruments survive (*New Langwill*).

                                D 14
MAKER                           Unknown: ?Hotteterre
DATES                           ?C19
LOCATION                        GB – London: Royal College of Music
COLLECTION NUMBER               88
TYPE                            Tenor
LENGTH                          710 mm
MATERIALS/MOUNTS                Stained wood: ivory mounts and bell-rim
KEYS                            1 swallow key
MARK                            resembles 5-pointed star
PROVENANCE                      ex Donaldson
SOURCES                         Lander: collection catalogue: Wells (personal
                                communication 1981): museum visit

Some authorities consider this instrument to be by one of the Hotteterre family who were active in La Couture-Boussey from the early seventeenth to the late eighteenth centuries. Hunt, however, writes that although the recorder resembles an Hotteterre recorder, the stamp is inconsistent with the family.[43] *New Langwill* illustrates a mark (star)/ HOTTETERRE, ascribing this possibly to Louis Hotteterre (c1645 – 1716) but the recorder under discussion does not bear the mark HOTTETERRE and is in the late baroque style.

A number of late-nineteenth century copies bear marks which are inconsistent with the originals (e.g. N40, A14, A18, A38-40, A43) and the museum staff consider this recorder to be of nineteenth-century origin.[44]

The present author examined the instrument in February 2003 and noted very little wear in the thumb hole, suggesting that the instrument had been little-used. There were clearly visible brush marks in the stain, concentric on the head but vertical on the middle joint, suggesting inferior workmanship. The instrument bears a superficial

---

[43] Hunt, E.H., 'A Hotteterre Tenor?', *Recorder and Music* IV 9 (1974), p227
[44] Wells, E. personal communication 1981

resemblance to other late nineteenth-century French tenor recorders preserved in Paris and La Couture.

A nineteenth-century origin seems likely.

|  | D 15 |
|---|---|
| MAKER | Unknown: ??METZLER |
| PLACE OF WORK | London (GB) |
| LOCATION | Unknown |
| TYPE | Voice flute |
| LOWEST NOTE | d' |
| MATERIALS/MOUNTS | Box: ivory mounts |
| MARK | METZLER/ LONDON/ 105.WARDOUR ST. |
| SOURCE | Luckett (personal communications 1981, 2003) |

The present author encountered this voice flute while it was being restored by Carl Dolmetsch in Haslemere around 1980, and it was discussing the instrument that aroused his interest in the history of the recorder in the nineteenth century. Dolmetsch considered that the recorder was likely to be of nineteenth-century origin, but others (notably its previous owner, Richard Luckett, and also Graham Wells) considered that it was probably an eighteenth-century instrument which had passed through Metzler's workshop for repair.

Metzler worked in Wardour Street, London between 1788 and 1815, and even if the recorder is of earlier manufacture the fact that it passed through Metzler's hands suggests that it was in use at the time. Three generations of the Metzler family were active in London and there is some doubt as to which family member the mark may be ascribed.

The recorder does not play in tune, which is perhaps the reason for its failure to sell at a recent London auction. Montagu comments:

> The failure [to sell] of the Metzler voice flute could well be blamed on the catalogue, which referred to the 'nineteenth-century family of makers' even though Valentine Metzler, the first of the family to settle here, was established in Wardour Street by 1788, a date which is late but not impossibly so for such an instrument...the instrument blew well and otherwise looked worth having as a genuine eighteenth-century recorder.[45]

It is most likely an eighteenth-century voice flute which continued to be used in the nineteenth century.

---

45  Montagu, J., Saleroom Report, *Early Music* XXX 1 (2002), pp149-152

|  |  |
|---|---|
|  | D 16 |
| MAKER | Unknown |
| DATE | ?C19 |
| LOCATION | US – DC – Washington – Smithsonian |
| COLLECTION NUMBER | 214487 |
| TYPE | Alto |
| LENGTH | 485 mm |
| MATERIALS/MOUNTS | Maple: ivory ferrules |
| PROVENANCE | ex Galpin |
| SOURCES | Sheldon (personal communication 1981) |

This instrument was acquired by the Smithsonian Collection from Galpin in 1902. It is described as being probably the work of an amateur or folk craftsman and could be of either eighteenth- or nineteenth-century origin.

|  |  |
|---|---|
|  | D 17 |
| MAKER | Unknown |
| DATE | Late C19 |
| PLACE OF WORK | London (GB) |
| LOCATION | GB – Oxford: Bate Collection |
| COLLECTION NUMBER | 0108 |
| TYPE | 'Improved patent voice flute' |
| MATERIALS/MOUNTS | Cocus: German silver ferrules |
| KEYS | 5: nickel-silver |
| MARK | (crown)/ IMPROVED/ PATENT/ VOICE/ FLUTE/ LONDON |
| SOURCES | la Rue (personal communication 2003): collection on-line catalogue: museum visit |

This instrument is included to highlight the terminological problems encountered in the organology of the recorder. The term 'voice flute' suggests a recorder in d' but this instrument is not a recorder, having no thumb hole: it is not a 'patent voice flute' for the instrument of that name for which Macgregor took out a patent in 1810 was a transverse alto flute with a hole bored in the head joint which was covered by a vibrating membrane (see comments on recorder N15). An example of this type of instrument is preserved in the Museum of Fine Arts, Boston (17.1857).

This instrument is an unclassified hybrid duct flute of the late nineteenth century.

### D18

| | |
|---|---|
| MAKER | FRENCH, George (GB) |
| DATES | fl 1840-1860 |
| PLACE OF WORK | London |
| LOCATION | US – MA – BOSTON: Museum of Fine Arts |
| COLLECTION NUMBER | 17.1839 |
| TYPE | Hybrid: see notes |
| LOWEST NOTE | d' |
| LENGTH | 555 mm |
| MATERIALS/MOUNTS | Varnished box: ivory mounts & bell-rim |
| KEYS | 1 closed key for RH 4 |
| MARK | FRENCH/LONDON |
| PROVENANCE | ex Leslie Lindsey Mason |
| SOURCE | Collection on-line catalogue |

4 pieces: conoidal bore: described as being 'in C'. The instrument resembles a traversa with a recorder head.

### D19

| | |
|---|---|
| MAKER | Unknown |
| DATES | See below |
| LOCATION | US – DC – Washington: DCM |
| COLLECTION NUMBER | 0860 |
| TYPE | Basset |
| LOWEST NOTE | g or a flat |
| MATERIALS/MOUNTS | Brass mounts |
| KEYS | 1 |
| SOURCE | Collection on-line catalogue: Lander |

Of questionable origin: part of the instrument may be C17 but most appears to have been crafted in C19 for decorative purposes. The finger groupings and placement appear to have been drilled for that purpose and perhaps from a fanciful iconographic source. There is a fontanelle in the manner of renaissance recorders.

### D20

| | |
|---|---|
| MAKER | Unknown |
| DATES | C19 |
| LOCATION | US – DC – Washington: DCM |
| COLLECTION NUMBER | 0907 |

| | |
|---|---|
| TYPE | Basset |
| LENGTH | 937 mm |
| MATERIALS/MOUNTS | Stained maple: brass mounts |
| KEYS | 1 |
| PROVENANCE | ex Opperman |
| SOURCE | Collection on-line catalogue: Lander |

Blown through a crook, with irregular placing of the finger-holes: most likely of C19 origin and fabricated for amateur collector sales.

### D21

| | |
|---|---|
| MAKER | AE |
| DATES | ?C19 |
| LOCATION | NL – Hague: Gemeentemuseum |
| TYPE | Alto |
| LOWEST NOTE | f' |
| LENGTH | 490 mm |
| MATERIALS/MOUNTS | Stained wood: ivory mounts |
| SOURCE | Lander |

### D22

| | |
|---|---|
| MAKER | Unknown |
| DATES | C19 |
| LOCATION | US – DC – Washington: DCM |
| COLLECTION NUMBER | 0325 |
| TYPE | Tenor |
| LOWEST NOTE | b flat (modern pitch) |
| LENGTH | 710 mm |
| MATERIALS/MOUNTS | Stained box: ivory mounts |
| KEYS | 1 |
| PROVENANCE | ex Tolbecque |
| SOURCE | Collection on-line catalogue |

The recorder bears a marked external similarity to Tolbecque's copy of an Hotteterre tenor in Le Musée de la Musique in Paris (E 2138, N55 in the present inventory [q.v.]).

### D23

| | |
|---|---|
| MAKER | Hawkes (firm of) (GB) |
| DATES | 1889 – 1930 |

## The Recorder In The Nineteenth Century

| | |
|---|---|
| PLACE OF WORK | London |
| LOCATION | GB – Stockport – Turner (private collection) |
| TYPE | Alto |
| LENGTH | c550 mm |
| MATERIALS/MOUNTS | Stained wood: metal mounts |
| KEYS | 4 |
| MAKER'S MARK | HAWKES & SON/DENMAN STREET/PICADILLY/LONDON |
| SOURCE | Turner (personal communication 2007) |

A four-piece recorder with a short clarinet-like bell. The firm of Hawkes was founded in 1860 and used the mark noted above from 1889. The firm merged with the revival company of Boosey in 1930 to form Boosey and Hawkes.

# CHAPTER IV

## THE RECORDERS DISCUSSED

The inventory gives as much detail as may be discerned about the individual recorders and points of interest are discussed on many of the instruments. The present chapter attempts to give an overview of the inventory in terms of the geographical location of the makers, the various types of recorder and other points worthy of more detailed collective organological study. The chapter will focus primarily on the named, anonymous, and 'early' groups of recorders (the N, A, and E series) representing the more orthodox instruments: the recorders forming the heterogenous group of the D series are mentioned briefly where this is relevant to the discussion, but many of these instruments do not fall into easily defined categories. In order to simplify the text, recorders smaller than the alto in f' will de described as 'small recorders', the vast majority of these being sixth flutes or fifth flutes (sopranos). Altos, voice flutes, and tenors will be styled 'medium-sized recorders', and bassets, basses and contrabasses identified as 'large recorders'

## LOCATION OF RECORDER MAKERS

Under this heading, only the recorders whose makers (and consequently town, country, and approximate date of manufacture) are identified will be discussed in detail: the origin of the anonymous instruments is too uncertain in most cases to be of substantial value in this respect. The instruments of the E series are included where relevant. Most of the recorders are of northern European origin, and four areas predominate, namely London, Paris and its environs, Bavaria/upper Austria and Brussels.

The recorders made in London date mainly from the early part of the nineteenth century and most were made by the firm of Goulding & Co., which traded under that name between 1798 and 1803: the instrument ascribed to Goulding & D'Almaine (D7) dates from the period 1813 – 1824. Of the Goulding & Co. instruments, four are altos and one is a tenor: the most common recorder in English use was the alto and the instruments by Goulding & Co. represent the end of the English recorder making tradition, for the German flute had all but usurped the recorder by the late eighteenth century. In addition, a solitary tenor by Oppenheim originated in London, a sixth flute by Townsend (N56) appeared in Manchester, and a soprano by Lamy (N22) was made in London but this instrument probably belongs to the early days of the recorder revival rather than to a continuing eighteenth-century tradition - unlike the other recorders discussed above.

There were two principal centres of recorder making in France: Paris and the Normandy villages of La Couture-Boussey and Ivry-la-Bataille. La Couture was the home of the Hotteterre family who were largely responsible for the evolution of the baroque recorder, and the village continued as a centre of woodwind instrument manufacture until the twentieth century, similar activity existing in Ivry-la-Bataille some four kilometres to the south-east. The French recorders essentially fall into two distinct classes, those of the continuing tradition and those of the recorder revival although some are difficult to place in either category: in the second group a number of instruments were made purely as exhibition pieces (*reconstitutions*) for the museum at La Couture. The Parisian instruments include not only instruments which appear to continue an old tradition (even if developed in detail) such as N1, N3, N4, N20 but also other anonymous recorders which are almost certainly related to the revival (A1-12) and the instrument by Colas (N5). This instrument is of similar external appearance to the alto by F.Noblet (N45) which may date from rather earlier in the century. The similarity of recorders N5 and N45 to five anonymous recorders has been alluded to in the inventory (see under A2): the particular shape of these instruments appears to be confined to French recorders. The anonymous instruments from La Couture are associated with the revival but it is not possible to allocate other French instruments to either category with any degree of certainty although it would generally be more appropriate to link them with the revival (for example, the sopranos by Gras (N18) and Lecomte (N23,24). The French instruments represent several types of recorder but, as in England, the medium-sized instruments predominate both in the continuing tradition of recorder making and in the instruments of the revival.

The types of recorder being built would be expected to give an indication of the use to which the instruments were put but little recorder music from the period survives in either England or France (see Chapter VI, 'Music for the Recorder'). However, a comparison with the next group, the recorders from Bavaria and upper Austria, provides an interesting contrast in terms of the types of recorders manufactured in that particular geographical location.

In the southern German state of Bavaria the recorder experienced a remarkable flowering in the first seventy years of the nineteenth century. If the area under consideration is widened to include the northern Austrian town of Schwaz, eighteen out of the sixty-eight N series instruments (together with four of the E series) were made in an area which measures a mere 160 km from north to south (including the towns of Nuremberg, Neuberg, and Schwaz) with the isolated town of Berchtesgaden (home of the Walch dynasty) lying 120 km to the east. Two other N series recorders (N51, 52) come from the Austrian town of Graz, around 200 km to the east of Berchtesgaden. Twelve of the Berchtesgaden instruments were made by Lorenz Walch II and his son Paul (N57-68), and a further four were made by Lorenz Walch II's father, Lorenz I, at the turn of the eighteenth and nineteenth centuries (E4-7). It is with regard to the type of instrument that the Bavarian recorders pose considerable interest, for out of the total of eighteen N series, fourteen are small recorders. It is apparent that this is in marked contrast to the French and English predominance of medium-sized instruments. Recorders have been made in Berchtesgaden since the sixteenth century, but the predominance of small recorders appears to be a nineteenth- century phenomenon, for a brief search for extant instruments made in the town before 1800 revealed a total of eighteen instruments, only five being small recorders. The Berchtesgaden tradition is discussed in Chapter V, 'The Berchtesgadner Fleitl'. Four altos (N25-28, by F II and J.A. Löhner) emanate from Nuremberg.

The existence of active schools of recorder-making in Bavaria and upper Austria in the mid to late nineteenth century (which is not paralleled in the remainder of Germany, Austria, or Switzerland) suggests a particular role for these (mainly small) recorders, and forms a contrast to the English and French preference for altos, tenors and the occasional voice flute.

The recorders made in Brussels are almost entirely associated with the revival of the instrument, fourteen out of fifteen being made (or caused to be made) by the pioneer organologist Victor-Charles Mahillon. The remaining Belgian instrument is an alto by Dupré (1790-1862, N6).

Few recorders were made in southern Europe in the nineteenth century: three in the checklist are of Italian origin (N11, E1,2) but no recorders have been found originating from the Iberian peninsula during the century.

## TYPES (SIZES) OF RECORDERS

The recorder family encompasses many sizes of instrument, ranging from the tiny Garklein Flötlein in c''' to the massive contrabass, an instrument which measures some two metres in length and whose lowest note is C: the more familiar instruments at the present time range from the sopranino in f" to the so-called great bass in c. At different periods in history particular recorders have been favoured, the choice reflecting contemporary repertoire. Of the sixty-eight N series recorders, twenty-eight are small, twenty-five medium, and ten large: the sizes of five are unknown. The preponderance of small recorders relates to the Bavarian tradition and, as has been indicated, is not consistent with the pattern expected from that displayed during the eighteenth century. Some of the recorders form part of a continued tradition of recorder making (such as the Berchtesgaden and Goulding instruments) whereas others are apparently associated with the recorder revival (for example, those by Galpin and Mahillon): some recorders cannot be placed in either category. In the 'traditional' group, there is a preponderance of small recorders over medium, this being explained by the large number of Bavarian sixth and fifth flutes. Of those associated with the revival, medium sized recorders predominate (with an unusually high proportion of tenors) yet a total of eight are large instruments. The relatively small proportion of altos in the medium-sized category is explained by an enthusiasm for the tenor recorder in France and the seemingly inappropriate number of large recorders explicable by an apparent fascination on the part of Mahillon for low recorders.

Out of the A series, fourteen are small recorders, twenty-three medium, and six large, with four of unknown type: these figures are less significant than those of the N series but do confirm the expected preponderance of medium-sized recorders by the presence of fifteen altos.

Five of the E series are small recorders, the remainder being altos.

In summary, out of the 124 recorders of the N, A, and E series, the sizes of nine are unknown: of the remainder, forty-seven are small recorders and forty-three are altos.

In this context it is appropriate to make a brief examination of the role of the recorder in the previous century in order to reveal changes in the pattern of recorder building and relate this to the use to which the instruments were put. The number of larger recorders declined substantially during the eighteenth century: tenors and basses (bassets) were essentially consort instruments but in the late seventeenth and eighteenth centuries compositional style had moved away from the consort music of the sixteenth and early seventeenth centuries towards the solo sonata, trio sonata and concerto repertoire. The vast majority of the late baroque repertoire was written for the alto recorder, this being reflected in the preponderance of alto recorders in collections: Halfpenny identified thirty-four altos out of a total of forty-three recorders in his survey of the English baroque treble (alto) recorder.[46] MacMillan commented that the repertoire for small recorders in the late baroque was extremely limited, comprising only a handful of concerti and a few obbligato passages.[47]

Given this historical background, the high proportion of small recorders in relation to altos is somewhat surprising, particularly when looking at those instruments of the N series which represent a continued tradition of recorder making: a continued – even if very limited – use of the instrument in a late eighteenth-century style would suggest that more altos would be found. The different sizes of recorder do, however, exhibit a differing geographical distribution in that the majority of fifth and sixth flutes come from Bavaria and upper Austria whereas more altos (in proportion) emanate from England and France: these points have been noted above but are reiterated here for convenience. It would be reasonable to speculate that these small recorders had a specific musical role in the region in which they were made and that this role differed from the historic role of the baroque recorder. The paucity of large recorders (with the exception of those copies made during the early years of the revival) reflects the changes in musical style which occurred throughout the eighteenth century and so requires no further comment.

---

46   Halfpenny, E., 'The English Baroque Treble Recorder', *Galpin Society Journal* IX (1956), pp82-90
47   MacMillan, D., 'The Descant Recorder in the early eighteenth Century', *Recorder and Music* VIII 1 (1981), pp12-13

## KEYS ON THE RECORDER

The recorder is essentially a keyless duct flute, with the chromatic scale being completed by a system of cross-fingering, although keys have often been added to larger instruments to bring the lowermost tone-hole(s) within easy reach of the player's fingers. Keys on woodwind instruments have three functions, the first, as noted above, being to bring certain holes within reach of the player's fingers, such a feature being found on large recorders from the time of Virdung's *Musica getutscht und ausgezogen* of 1511. Secondly, keys allow a finger to occlude more than one tone-hole and thus simplify the cross-fingering required to produce a chromatic scale: this has not been a tradition in the history of the recorder. Thirdly, keys may serve to increase the upward or downward range of the instrument. Some nineteenth-century recorders were fitted with keys (probably in an attempt to develop the instrument in parallel with the orchestral woodwinds) and in more modern times attempts have been made both to simplify the fingering of the notes in the third octave and to extend the compass of the instrument by means of keys but this practice has not gained widespread acceptance.

Few recorders have extensive keywork and, out of the current N series, only six are worthy of comment. The French recorders by Bellissent and Jeantet (N1, N20) are both tenors, the Bellissent having seven keys and the Jeantet, the head of which is lost, six. Both instruments were made at a similar date but in different towns and there is no similarity in the pattern of keywork: these instruments represent attempts on the part of the maker to introduce keyed recorders but may have been made for specific customers as neither man appears to have made other recorders. The so-called 'treble in a' by Kruspe (N21) has four keys, an unusual feature on recorders of this size: Kruspe, however, was an experimenter and made several improvements to the transverse flute. An alto by Dupré (N6) has two keys. The sixth flute by Schweffer (N51) has one key (for the little finger of the right hand), this feature being most unusual on small recorders. The other instruments in the N series which have keys (ten) are all tenors, bassets, or basses, many being reproductions of old recorders: this is unremarkable.

Of the A series, fourteen have keys. Most are tenors and basses but two German instruments (A26, A27) have six keys. One is a soprano, the other an alto but both exhibit the same pattern of keywork: the keys are of German silver and both are of German origin, possibly by the same maker who may have been intent on developing the instrument. There is also a large three-keyed alto in the Gemeentemuseum in The Hague (A30) and the lost large alto by Grenser (E3) possessed three keys for the lowest semitones. It is difficult to draw conclusions from the keywork on the less-conventional instruments making up the D series for these instruments represent – in the main – a series of 'one-off' curiosities.

Most –indeed all – orchestral woodwind instruments acquired more extensive keywork during the late eighteenth and early nineteenth centuries: the flute underwent transformation from the simple d sharp key of the baroque flute to the complex fully-keyed instrument of Boehm in a mere 100 years, and the oboe, clarinet and bassoon became increasingly complex in order to simplify fingering and improve intonation over the chromatic compass of the instrument. The question therefore arises as to why the addition of keys to the recorder was – and indeed is – manifestly unpopular. The answer, I believe, is that by the time extensive and good-quality key mechanisms were developed, the recorder had become obsolescent, certainly as far as serious art music was concerned and it no longer had an orchestral use. Those few musicians who wished to continue to play the recorder were no doubt content to wrestle with its complex cross-fingerings, which, in themselves, contribute to the unique veiled tone of the instrument. The few soprano and alto recorders with keywork were no more than experiments, and, like so many experiments in the history of the development of musical instruments, were rapidly consigned to history.

## THE FOOT-JOINT

The majority of the recorders surveyed (excepting the copies of renaissance instruments) exhibit the classical turned foot-joint of the baroque recorder but a small number have straight foot-joints or clarinet-like bells.

The straight foot-joint bears an external similarity to flutes of the period, and is first encountered in some of the recorders by Thomas Stanesby junior (1692-1754), a fine example being the four-jointed tenor in Le Musée de la Musique in Paris (E. 980.2.86). Such foot-joints are most common on English instruments and may be seen on the Goulding tenor N15 (Illustration I): in addition to the Goulding instruments, the straight foot joint is found on the tenor by Oppenheim (N49) and on the sixth flute by Townsend (N56). The bore of this joint on N15 is conical, whereas that of the foot of flutes of the period is usually cylindrical. Although most common on English recorders, the keyed French instrument by Jeantet (N20) has a straight foot with a key for the little finger of the right hand. The significance of the straight foot appears to be more aesthetic than functional.

Six recorders in the checklist have clarinet-like bells: the keyed tenor by Bellissent (N1), the lost alto by Grenser (E3), the four-keyed alto by Kruspe (N21) and the two German *Langsflöten* A25, 26, together with the Hawkes alto D23. A number of csakans had clarinet-like bells, and it is possible that the makers of the recorders cited above were attempting to develop the acoustical properties of the instrument by enhancing the lower register and thus produce a more even volume of tone throughout its compass. The bell-ended recorder appears to have been another experiment of the nineteenth century which was not pursued in the twentieth-century development of the instrument.

## RECORDERS WITH A SPONGE CHAMBER

Condensation of moisture in the windway, leading to 'clogging' and difficulty with tone production, has long been a problem for recorder players and the sponge chamber of the flageolet represents an attempt to alleviate this difficulty. The sponge chamber, a space between the mouthpiece and the sound-producing labium and window, is not a feature of the recorder but forms an integral part of the recorder's cousin, the flageolet, wherein it serves to contain a sponge to absorb moisture from the player's breath. By passing through a sponge, the force of the player's breath is considerably diminished by the time it reaches the sound-producing mechanism and the tone is, in consequence, softened.

Three recorders in the checklist exhibit this feature. The first is the tenor by Goulding (N15), the second, the composite instrument by Boie (D3) which has separate recorder and flageolet heads, and the third, the flageolet-like instrument by Firth, Pond & Co. (D5).

## WOODS USED FOR RECORDERS

Over the centuries, many different timbers have been utilized in the manufacture of recorders and a glance at any current maker's catalogue will reveal that both hard and soft woods remain available. The harder and more dense woods (such as rosewood and the blackwoods) produce a more robust tone, the softer fruitwoods being more suited to consort playing. In former centuries exotic hardwoods from tropical countries were less readily available in Europe and makers tended to rely on indigenous species, notably boxwood and the fruitwoods.

Discounting those instruments of the N series definitely associated with the recorder revival and whose type of timber is known, the majority of the remainder are of box, with plumwood being the next most popular wood. A similar pattern is seen in the recorders of the E series. Of the hardwoods, palisander (a Brazilian rosewood) is the most common, with a few instruments being made of blackwood. The boxwood recorders are distributed throughout Europe but all the plumwood instruments emanate from Bavaria and northern Austria. Of the twelve Berchtesgaden recorders in the N series, five are of box and four of plum and the four by Lorenz Walch I in the E series are also of plum. The A series exhibits a mixed distribution of timbers, with no pattern being discernable: however, the fourth flute of probable Berchtesgaden origin (A24) is of plum.

Boxwood (*Buxus sempervirens*) is an evergreen tree formerly widespread in southern Europe, England and the Middle East: it is noteworthy for its ease of turning and carving, its light colour aiding the craftsman. It was the most popular wood used in the manufacture of woodwind instruments from the seventeenth to the nineteenth centuries. Plum (*Prunus domesticus*) is a moderately hard wood grown in southern Europe, having a fine, smooth texture. It is less dense than box, having a density of 0.9 – 1.2 grams per cubic centimetre whereas plum has a density of only 0.6 – 0.8 and the hardwoods circa1.5.

Box appears to have been the favoured wood for making recorders. The name of the French village of La Couture-Boussey, one of the centres of woodwind instrument making from the seventeenth to the nineteenth centuries, is derived from the French word for box (*buis*) a particularly prevalent tree in the area. Plum is widely-grown in south-central Europe, and appears to have been particularly favoured by the Bavarian and Austrian makers, no doubt on account of its ready availability, exotic hardwoods being expensive and difficult to obtain in the land-locked countries of central Europe. Instrument makers, on the whole, pragmatically chose a suitable local timber if one was available.

## MAKER'S MARKS

Maker's marks provide the organologist with information not only about the maker of an instrument but also may give clues as to the approximate date of manufacture, for some makers modified their marks as time progressed. In the present context, two aspects are worthy of consideration, these being pitch marks and maker's marks on reproduction instruments associated with the recorder revival.

In a chapter on maker's marks in Waterhouse's *The New Langwill Index,* Heyde comments that marks may be found on both woodwind and brass instruments to indicate the pitch of the instrument and notes that this practice was particularly common in the eighteenth and nineteenth centuries.[48] Pitch marks are usually stamped in close proximity to the maker's mark and indicate the lowest note of the instrument: they are particularly prevalent on the Bavarian and upper Austrian recorders (Illustration II: recorder N58). Recorders bearing pitch marks in the present inventory are listed below.

| D | C | B | A |
| --- | --- | --- | --- |
| N50 | N58 | A24 | N62 |
| N51 | N59 | | |
| N57 | N61 | | |
| N60 | N66 | | |
| N65 | N67 | | |

N60 is stamped D but Young gives c" as the lowest note. The mark 'B' on A24 has aided its identification as an instrument of the Berchtesgaden school, and N62 is pitched in a' flat. The figure '6' appears on the small recorder by Townsend (N56) suggesting that it may be a sixth flute.

---

48   Heyde, H., in *The New Langwill Index,* ppxiii-xxxviii

A feature which has not hitherto been deemed worthy of comment is the 'authenticity' of maker's marks on a number of the recorders associated with the recorder revival. In the course of the inventory it has been noted that the marks on some copies of old instruments do not agree with the marks of the original maker (N40, A14, A18, A38 - 40) or lend doubt as to the maker (D14). In particular, the controversy surrounding the maker of the three renaissance recorders A38 - 40 (unknown, possibly Kynseker or Mahillon) *may* be resolved by the observation that Mahillon's copy of a bass by Rauch (N40) bears a mark inconsistent with that maker, and this observation may lend credence to the notion that Mahillon was the maker of A38 - 40 as these recorders also bear unauthentic maker's marks. The probable explanation for the lack of authenticity of marks on the copies is that at the time they were made, the concept of absolute accuracy in copying old instruments was far from advanced and the makers simply stamped an appropriate name without further research into details of the original mark.

## THE E SERIES

This small series of nine recorders represents a group of instruments made in the late eighteenth or early nineteenth centuries, their makers being active in the eighteenth century but dying in the early years of the nineteenth. Beyond illustrating a link between the recorder makers of the high baroque period and the sporadic makers of the nineteenth century they are of little interest although it is worthy of note that the instruments of Lorenz Walch I represent a continued family tradition in that both his father (Georg) and son (Lorenz II) were recorder makers.

## THE D SERIES

The instruments in this category form a collection of both typical and atypical recorders which, for one reason or another, cannot be classified in any other series in the inventory. Some are included because their whereabouts are not known or details of their maker is uncertain, others because they are not typical recorders, and yet others because the date of their manufacture cannot be ascertained with any degree of accuracy. Each instrument is discussed in the inventory. Taken overall, the D series of recorders serves to illustrate a combination of a continuing tradition of recorder making, nineteenth-century experimentation and some early incursions into reviving the recorder. Many of the instruments are the subject of either doubt or controversy (hence their classification) but are included in the present work not only as further evidence that interest in the recorder continued during the nineteenth century but also as evidence that attempts were being made to develop the instrument even during the dark days of its history.

## RECORDERS ASSOCIATED WITH THE REVIVAL

Some of the instruments in the inventory represent the 'tail end' of the baroque tradition (e.g. the instruments by Goulding), others, notably the Berchtesgaden recorders, a continued but altering tradition, whereas others are clearly associated with the revival of the recorder. Many instruments are difficult to place in any of the above categories because they appear to date from around the middle of the nineteenth century or because there is insufficient evidence to align them with any particular group.

The reasons underlying the revival are explored in subsequent chapters and it suffices to say – for the present – that by the 1880s considerable interest was being expressed in both the music and the instruments of the renaissance and baroque periods. By 1881 Mahillon had made (or caused to be made) reproductions of the renaissance contrabass in Antwerp (N41, ?A43) and in 1885 his copies of the Nuremberg Kynseker recorders were played at the International Inventions Exhibition in London (N31 - 38). Most of Mahillon's recorders were copies of renaissance instruments, as were those of the English antiquarian Galpin (N7-10), both makers assembling complete consorts of recorders and using them in performance. Gerlach and Tolbecque copied baroque recorders (N12, N55).

The recorders of the A series are inevitably more difficult to place in terms of their dates of manufacture, but some of these instruments may be definitively aligned with the revival. The reproductions made in La Couture-Boussey date from the period 1888-96: some of these were made for museum display only (A15, A16, A19, A20). It is likely that many of the anonymous instruments in La Cité de la Musique (A1 - 12) are also connected with the revival, and attention has been drawn in the inventory to the external similarity between A2, A6, A7, A34, A35 together with the lost instrument illustrated by Hipkins to the recorder N5 by Colas and also to the alto by F.Noblet (N45). The subject of the French recorders and their place in the revival is further discussed under the heading 'The recorder revival in France' in Chapter IX. The three German recorders in the Carl Claudius Collection in Copenhagen (A25 - 27) were described as 'modern' German *Langsflöten* when acquired by the museum in 1900 and therefore are probably related to the revival. A38 - 40 and A42 in The Metropolitan Museum of Art, New York, are also reproductions.

It is apparent from the inventory that many of the instruments dating from the early days of the revival are of the renaissance type, but it is difficult to ascertain the reasons for this. It might be expected that the baroque recorder, only out of common use for a century, would have been the first to be copied as both the instruments and their repertoire are more prevalent in collections, but it may be that the renaissance instruments were copied in an attempt to return to the music of a much earlier age in parallel with the Pre-Raphaelite movement in art and the gothic revival in architecture. This is, at present, pure conjecture, there being as yet no evidence available to substantiate the hypothesis.

The manufacture of copies of old recorders in the late nineteenth century heralded the vast expansion of recorder making in the second quarter of the twentieth century: the very existence of these early copies testifies not only to the growing interest in early music as the nineteenth century drew to its close, but also to the dismissal of the widely-held notion that Arnold Dolmetsch was the first to make recorders at the very dawn of its new age. By the time Dolmetsch had made his first recorder, those of Victor-Charles Mahillon were some forty years old.

## CONCLUSION

Certain conclusions may be drawn from the inventory and discussion, the former demonstrating in itself both the continued and revived use of the recorder between 1800 and 1905.

1. Recorders continued to be made in small numbers throughout the nineteenth century.

2. Many of the recorders bear maker's marks, rendering it possible to identify geographical patterns in recorder making, with particular activity in London, Paris and Bavaria/northern Austria. Later in the nineteenth century, Brussels, Paris, La Couture-Boussey and Ivry-la-Bataille were associated with the manufacture of copies of historic recorders.

3. In the nineteenth century the recorder was largely confined to northern Europe.

4. In the eighteenth century alto recorders predominated, but out of 124 recorders in the N, A, and E series of the inventory of nineteenth-century recorders the majority are small recorders, closely followed by altos. This curious disparity is explained by the large number of small recorders (principally fifth and sixth flutes) emanating from the Bavarian / northern Austrian tradition, for elsewhere there remains a preponderance of alto recorders. There are relatively few tenors and very few bassets or basses.

5. A number of experiments were made in recorder design, notably in the use of keys and modification of the foot of the instrument. The nineteenth century was a period of intense experimentation in the design of musical instruments and it is hardly surprising that the recorder should have been a subject for such practice. However, the experiments and modifications to the recorder were ephemeral.

6. Several unusual recorders or recorder-type instruments were made and are described in the D series of the inventory.

7. A number of makers began to make copies of old recorders during the final twenty years of the nineteenth century, the practice accelerating in the early twentieth century. Some of these instruments were made solely for the purpose of museum display, whilst others were playable copies, made with varying degrees of historical veracity. Such activity related to the rediscovery of, and interest in, early music and prefigured the work of later makers whose names are familiar as pillars of the recorder revival.

8. The maker's mark on some of the copies of historic recorders does not always accurately reflect the original maker's mark (as is current practice) and this should be borne in mind when ascribing a date to the instruments in question.

# CHAPTER V

## THE BERCHTESGADNER FLEITL

The Bavarian resort town of Berchtesgaden lies in the valley of the Berchtesgaden stream and is surrounded by mountains, the 'landmark' of the town being the twin-peaked Watzmann. It is some 120 km east-south-east of Munich and around 25 km from Mozart's home town of Salzburg, and perhaps best known to the tourist as the site of Hitler's 'Eagle's Nest', his mountain retreat from the rigours of government in Berlin. Berchtesgaden's isolation, however, belies its unique significance in the history of the recorder.

The Berchtesdgadner Fleitl is a baroque-style recorder of small size (hence the diminutive term *Fleitl*, meaning 'little flute') which appears to have arisen in the late eighteenth and early nineteenth centuries and whose manufacture continues to the present day, the end-product of many centuries of recorder making in Berchtesgaden. In Berchtesgaden the recorder *never* became extinct, a phenomenon unique in the history of the instrument for the continued existence of the Berchtesgaden school of recorder making now demonstrates that the recorder has a continuous history from the *Dordrecht* recorder of the early fifteenth century to the modern recorders of the twenty-first century, a history with few parallels in Western organology. A wood-turning industry has existed in Berchtesgaden since around the year 1100, and a guild of flute makers was established in 1581: for the purposes of the present study, however, it necessary to give particular attention to the families of Walch and Oeggl, the nineteenth century recorders of the Walch family representing a continued tradition of recorder making dating back to the seventeenth century until the death of Paul Walch in 1873 whereas members of the Oeggl dynasty have been making recorders from the late seventeenth or early eighteenth century to the present day.

### THE WALCH FAMILY

The Walch family was active in world of recorder making for over 300 years and some 50 members are documented in this respect, but it is only the last three generations which are of interest in the late history of the recorder. Bruckner gives a family tree,[49] and documents the surviving instruments (including recorders) of eight members of the family.[50]

Lorenz Walch I was born in Berchtesgaden in 1735 and was qualified as *ein Flautenmeistermacher* (master flute maker): a number of his instruments are extant

---

49  Bruckner, H., 'Die Pfeifenmacher Walch in Berchtesgaden', *Sänger und Musiktanzenzeitung* II (1978), pp55-66
50  Bruckner, H., 'Die Pfeifenmacherei in Berchtesgaden', *Tibia* II (1979), pp289-296

*The Recorder In The Nineteenth Century*

including four recorders (E4-7) and these bear the stamp

                L:WALCH /(in scroll) / (palmette)

There is however, some controversy over this mark (see below).

The third son of his parents, Lorenz Walch II was born in 1786 and also became a *Flautenmeistermacher* and owner of a property known as Rosspointlehens in the Stangasse, some two kilometres from the centre of Berchtesgaden. The house no longer exists but the area is clearly signed and is now the site of a small Marian shrine. In 1809 Lorenz II married Maria Hell, with whom he had ten children: six of the children followed the Berchtesgaden tradition of wood carving, one (Lorenz III 1811-1881) becoming a turner and one (Johann Paul 1810-1873) an instrument maker.

At least eight of Lorenz II's recorders are extant (N57-64) and bear one of the stamps

            (5 petal flower) / LORENZ WALCH / BERCHTESGADEN

            LORENZ / BERCHTESGADEN / (4 leafed clover)

            LORENZ BERCHTESGADEN / (5 leafed symbol)

Lorenz II and Johann Paul (known as Paul) were the only children of Lorenz to be involved in the history of the recorder, Lorenz opening a business with Paul in the Hablergasse (close to the market place) for selling their wares. Zimmerman considers the mark 'L:WALCH' to be that of Lorenz III, whereas Bruckner believes that Lorenz III was not an instrument maker and that the mark was that of his grandfather Lorenz I, a view with which Waterhouse (in *New Langwill*) and Helm concur.[51][52] I have accepted the consensus of opinion expressed by Bruckner and ascribe the mark to Lorenz I.

Paul (born 1810) inherited the house at Rosspointlehens upon his brother's death and continued the recorder making tradition. His mark

            (seven pointed star)/PAUL WALCH / BERCHTESGADEN / (rosette)

changed around 1850 to

            (crown) / PAUL WALCH / BERCHTESGADEN

---

51   Zimmermann, J., 'Die Pfeifenmacherfamilie Walch in Berchtesgaden', supplement to the *Berchtesgadener Anzeiger* (11 August 1937), pp21-24

52   Helm, A., *Das Berchtesgadener Land in Wandel der Zeit*, Berchtesgaden (1929) [page number and publisher unknown: photocopy in author's possession]

*The Berchtesgadner Fleitl*

following a visit of King Ludwig of Bavaria to the town but it is not known if the change was instigated as a result of a royal commission. Paul was the last of the Walch family to make recorders, and died in 1873. Four of his recorders are extant (N65-68) together with flutes, clarinets and a cane flute. A portrait photograph of Paul dated 1867 hangs in the Heimatmuseum in Berchtesgaden and is reproduced here: the instrument he holds appears to be a small clarinet. No other portrait of a nineteenth-century recorder maker is known to exist and this image forms a remarkable link in the chain of events surrounding the recorder in its dark age. Two sons of Lorenz II (Michael and Johann-Baptist) had studied photography and it is tempting to speculate that they were responsible for the portrait of their brother, for photographers were few and far between in the 1860s.

As time wore on, the number of instrument makers in Berchtesgaden declined rapidly from twenty-two in 1805 to a mere nine in 1847. Although last of the Walch dynasty, Paul's craft was not lost for he passed his skills to Georg Oeggl (1851-1929), thus ensuring the future of the centuries-old unbroken tradition of recorder making in Berchtesgaden.

Paul Walch

*The Recorder In The Nineteenth Century*

## THE OEGGL FAMILY

The woodwind instrument maker Peter Eggl worked in Berchtesgaden in the eighteenth century (a recorder survives in the Germanisches Nationalmuseum in Nuremberg) and the name appears to have undergone transformation to Ögl (or Öcl – this mark appearing on a recorder in the Museo Carolino Augusteum in Salzburg). These makers were active in Ettenburg from 1580 and in Klaushäusl in the Bischofswiesen district of Berchtesgaden by 1730: Bernard Oeggl continues to make recorders (Berchtesgadner Fleitln) at this location. In a personal communication to the author in 2003 Herr Oeggl wrote that his grandfather (Georg Oeggl, 1851-1929) had learnt the craft of flute (i.e. recorder) making from Paul Walch and he in turn passed his skills on to his grandson, also named Georg (1916-1996). Georg the younger taught the present maker of Berchtesgadner Fleitln, Bernard Oeggl (b1949), who is now the sole maker of the instrument. An article in the *Berchtesgadener Anzeiger* of 1997 outlined the materials and techniques employed in the building of Oeggl's instruments (plum with horn mounts, the traditional materials for the Berchtesgaden recorders) which are built in the key of C.[53] An example lies alongside recorders by the Walch dynasty in the Heimatmuseum at Berchtesgaden to illustrate the continuity of the tradition (Illustration V).

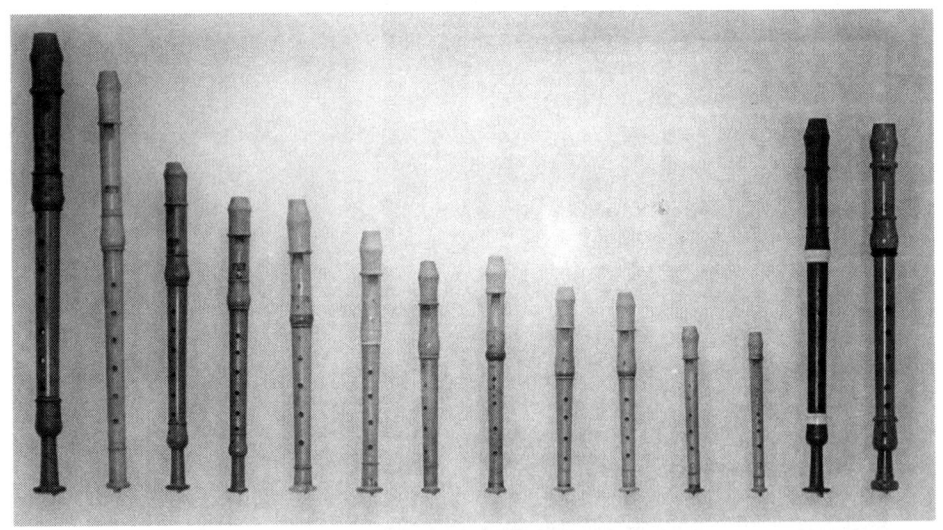

Berchtesgadner Fleitln and flageolets by Lorenz Walch I and II
Comtemporary Berchtesgadner Fleitl by Oeggl (Far right)
Author's photograph

---

53   Elch, I.C.H., 'Millimeterarbeit, die Ruhe und Liebe erforder', *Berchtesgadener Anzeiger* (June 1997)

## PLAIKNER

The name Plaikner appears in the literature concerning the Fleitl. This family worked in the town as *Pfeifenmachern* (pipe makers) at the turn of the seventeenth and eighteenth centuries but they appear unconnected with the later recorder making tradition.

## THE INSTRUMENTS

The Berchtesgadner [sic] Fleitl as it existed in the nineteenth century and as it exists today is a small recorder, essentially of baroque form. The instruments by Lorenz II and Paul Walch are almost all fifth or sixth flutes (there is a third flute by Lorenz II) but the modern instruments made by Oeggl are fifth flutes (sopranos). The Fleitl exhibits a characteristic form (particularly of the foot-joint) which is seen clearly in the Illustration of the Lorenz II recorder in the Dayton C. Miller Flute Collection in Washington (DCM 0663: N59). The preponderance of small recorders in Berchtesgaden and the surrounding areas is an unusual phenomenon and a brief search of Berchtesgaden recorders made prior to the nineteenth century revealed (as would be expected) a preponderance of altos and tenors.

| | | |
|---|---|---|
| Plaikner | c1696-1708 | 3 altos |
| P. Eggl | early C18 | 1 alto |
| A. Walch | early C18 | 1 sopranino   1 alto |
| Georg Walch | early C18 | 5 tenors |
| I.G. Walch | early C18 | 2 sixth flutes |
| Öcl | late C18 | 1 recorder (size unknown) |
| L. Walch I | 1735-1809 | 1 sopranino   1 sixth flute   1 alto |

Out of a total of eighteen, the sizes of five are known, there being seven altos and five tenors, leaving only five small recorders.

The change in size of the instrument from the baroque (when altos predominated) suggests a change in the use of the recorders, this trend being paralleled elsewhere in Bavaria and northern Austria.

## THE USE OF THE BERCHTESGADNER FLEITL

At present this matter remains conjectural as no music specifying the instrument has been discovered. The Berchtesgaden recorders of the eighteenth century appear to be of the type in common use in baroque music with its concerto, sonata and obbligato repertoire, whereas those of the nineteenth century appear inappropriate for 'art music' of the period and it would seem probable that the instrument underwent a gradual change of use from art music to folk music. In a telephone conversation in 2002, Oeggl advised me that the Fleitl was essentially used in folk music at the present time: in former times much of this repertoire would have been handed down by an aural tradition rather than upon the printed page, which would go at least some way towards explaining the apparent lack of repertoire for the instrument in the nineteenth century. It seems that the Berchtesgaden instruments progressed from altos and tenors to fifth and sixth flutes (albeit with a two octave chromatic compass) before being relegated to the realm of folk music: to make this assertion is not in any sense to denigrate the substantial art and skill of folk musicians - it is to highlight the evolution of a very particular variety of recorder.

## FLÖTEN-SCHULE UND LÄNDLER AUS BERCHTESGADEN

A booklet bearing the above title was published by the *Fachschule für Holzschnitzerei* (School of Woodcarving) in Berchtesgaden around the year 1900, the cover of the booklet depicting a young man lying in a meadow playing a recorder-type instrument with his right hand uppermost. The twin peaks of the Watzmann mountain form a backdrop to the scene but it is difficult to discern details of the instrument from the photocopy in the author's possession. A fingering chart is given which includes only the diatonic notes of the scale of C major, the compass ranging from c" to e"". There is no indication of the use of the 'pinched' thumb-hole for the second octave, but from e''' the indication *hier starker blasen* (here blow harder) is given and for the very high e"" the instruction *hier stark blasen* (here blow hard) is written. It is curious that the fingering includes only the diatonic scale, for the traditional Berchtesgaden instruments of the Walchs are fully chromatic, but it should be noted that some of the English eighteenth-century treatises included a fingering chart for the diatonic scale on the first pages, including chromatic fingerings only as the player advanced in technique. Alternative explanations may be that the tutor was intended for very elementary players who wished to play only the simplest of folk tunes, or that the booklet was not a tutor for the Berchtesgadner Fleitl but for another form of simple duct flute. A number of duct flutes of minor importance existed around the turn of the nineteenth and twentieth centuries: Zimmermann's catalogue (Leipzig c1900) illustrates simple 'csakans' with and without keys, but these differ from the classical

Viennese csakan described in Chapter I.[54] Various forms of the *Schulflöte* (some with only six finger-holes) existed in Germany in the first thirty years of the twentieth century but the terminology of these flutes and csakans is far from consistent. At best, the *Flöten-Schule* illustrates a continuation of the Berchtesgaden duct flute tradition.

The Berchtesgadner Fleitl occupies a unique place in the history of the recorder. Although the present-day descendants of the Bavarian baroque recorders have essentially become folk instruments, it has now been shown not only that the craft of recorder making continued in Berchtesgaden into the late nineteenth century but also that the recorder – in Berchtesgaden at least – never became extinct, and, through the Berchtesgaden story, that the recorder has existed in unbroken continuity from the fifteenth to the twenty-first century.

---

54  Betz, M., *Der Csakan und seine Musik*, p48

*The Recorder In The Nineteenth Century*

# CHAPTER VI

## MUSIC AND TREATISES FOR THE RECORDER

### MUSIC

In 1956 Carl Dolmetsch observed that a number of recorders had been made in the late eighteenth and early nineteenth centuries and posed the question ' for whom were these recorders made and what was played on them?'[55] Half a century later the question is still difficult to answer, for little music from the nineteenth century specifying the recorder has come to light. A search of the literature, modern publishers' catalogues (seeking modern editions of nineteenth century pieces) and correspondence with international scholars was substantially unproductive in discovering nineteenth-century compositions for the recorder, but the activities of Weber, Berlioz and J.C. Schultze in relation to the instrument are worthy of comment.

### WEBER

Recorders figured twice in the career of Carl Maria von Weber (1786-1826): firstly, the composer scored for two recorders in his youthful opera *Peter Schmoll und seine Nachbar* and, secondly, Weber heard two recorders at a concert in 1806. The opera *Peter Schmoll und seine Nachbar* (Peter Schmoll and his neighbour) was adapted from a novel by Carl Gottlieb Cramer with libretto by Joseph Turk; it was written by the young Weber under the eye of Michael Haydn in Salzburg and was probably given in Augsburg in 1803. A Terzetto (No.14) is scored for a pair of recorders, a pair of basset horns, bassoon, strings and bass soloist. Warrack quotes Weber as recounting:

> An article in a music paper awoke in me the idea of writing in another manner, of bringing back into use old and forgotten instruments.[56]

In 1806 the composer again encountered recorders whilst attending a performance of his *Kleiner Tusch* (Little Flourish) for twenty trumpets at a concert in Carlsruhe. During the concert he heard pieces performed on two badly-played recorders (*zwey schlecht geblässenen Flöte doucen*) and it has been suggested by Moeck that Weber had scored for

---

[55] Dolmetsch, C.F., 'The Recorder and German Flute during the seventeenth and eighteenth Centuries', *Proceedings of the Royal Musical Association* LXXXIII (1956), pp49-63

[56] Warrack, J., *Carl Maria von Weber*, (London: Hamish Hamilton 1968), p45

*The Recorder In The Nineteenth Century*

the recorder in his *Kleiner Tusch* but an examination of the score reveals that the piece is scored solely for trumpets with typical 'fanfare' passages (47a in Jähn's Catalogue of the works of Carl Maria von Weber).

## BERLIOZ

Hector Berlioz (1803-1869) published his sacred trilogy *L'enfance du Christ* in 1854 but it is known that he had worked on parts of the score for some years prior to the work's eventual publication. *L'adieu des bergers à la Sainte Famille* (from Part II of the trilogy *La fuite en Egypte* and popularly known as *The Shepherds' Farewell*) was originally an organ piece but subsequently was performed as a choral composition. For reasons which are not altogether clear, Berlioz ascribed the work to a fictitious seventeenth-century choirmaster of La Sainte Chapelle whom he named Pierre Ducré. Lloyd-Jones writes that the autograph score of the work lists a number of historic instruments, including flûtes douces, oboes, oboes da caccia, and chalumeaux, but there is no evidence that this scoring was ever used in performance.[57] The relevant parts are now scored for oboes and clarinets (Example I) but, interestingly, sound well when played on alto and tenor recorders. It would appear that Berlioz was cultivating a pastoral image by using the old instruments: given his interest in orchestration, he may have been aware of the eighteenth-century use of the recorder in such a context, but is known that he disliked the flageolet.

## L'Adieu des Bergers à la Sainte Famille

---

57  Lloyd-Jones, D., *Hector Berlioz. A new Edition of the Complete Works*, (Kassel: Bärenreiter 1998), Vol. II pviii

## SCHULTZE

Works ascribed to Johann Christoph Schultze (1733-1813) are often considered to be amongst the last written for the recorder before its apparent demise at the end of the eighteenth century and are thought to date from the late eighteenth or very early nineteenth century: as such, they are worthy of critical comment. All that is known of Schultze is that he was conductor of the orchestra at the Doebbelinscher Theater in Berlin from about 1768. Schultze's works for the recorder (no other compositions appear to be extant) include a concerto and a set of six suites for two recorders and continuo but doubt has been cast upon the authorship of these pieces. The concerto in G (for alto and strings) is written in three movement form and utilizes almost the entire compass of the recorder in f' (g' to g'''): the six suites are in the classical form of the French suite with an extended overture followed by a string of dances. Lasocki[58] suggested that the pieces may not have been composed by Schultze, but by Pierre Prowo (1697-1757) yet the matter remains unresolved at the time of writing. Examination of the music itself, however, yields clues as to the probable date of composition; the concerto is orchestrated in a style common in the late baroque, with the solo recorder sometimes accompanied by the upper strings, sometimes by the continuo, and sometimes by the whole ensemble. The suites are typical of early eighteenth-century French suites and it should be recalled that both the suite and trio sonata with *basso continuo* became less popular after the middle of the century. Professor Sebastian Forbes studied the harmony of parts of the d minor suite and formed the opinion that the style was likely to be that of a lesser German composer of the late baroque period.[59] Although the works of Schultze may be amongst the last to be composed for the recorder in the eighteenth century, there is little evidence to suggest that they are of nineteenth – or even late eighteenth – century origin.

## PARRY

John Turner recently published an article on 'John Parry's Nightingale' wherein he discusses a nineteenth-century concert piece for duct flute by the woodwind player and composer John Parry (1776-1851).[60] The title advertises the piece as 'The Nightingale,/A favourite MILITARY AIR Arranged as a /Rondo/for the /Piano Forte/with an accompaniment for the /Flute or Flageolet, '[etc.]. The composer (who played the piece on a flageolet) made the observation that 'Most of the upper lines may be played an octave higher on the flute' to which Turner adds a cautionary note but indicates that the piece could well be played on a soprano recorder. I would comment that, just because a piece is playable on the

---

58 Lasocki, D., 'Flute and Recorder in Combination', *Recorder and Music* IV/11 (1974), pp391-395
59 Forbes, S., personal communication, March 2003
60 Turner, J., 'John Parry's Nightingale', *The Recorder Magazine* XXV 1 (2005), PP13-15

*The Recorder In The Nineteenth Century*

recorder, it does not imply that this instrument was ever in the mind of the composer: the popular works of James Hook form a classic example. The significance of Parry's piece lies not in the potential use of the recorder, but in the uncommon use of the flageolet (a more popular duct flute than the recorder in Parry's time) in this particular context. Further nineteenth-century pieces specifying a flageolet as an accompanying instrument are now coming to light, but, at the time of writing, there is no evidence for the specific use of the recorder in this role.

## MUSIC FOR THE CSAKAN AND FLAGEOLET

Both the csakan and flageolet are 'soprano' duct flutes (see Chapter I) with a compass of a little over two octaves and much of their repertoire may be adapted for recorder(s). During its brief career the csakan acquired a repertoire of around 400 pieces and the flageolet (in its several forms) attracted the attention of composers. The dispute over whether *flûte douce* applies to the csakan or recorder (or both) is discussed in Chapter I but, regardless of the niceties of academic nomenclature, much csakan music is now played on recorders and it would not be inopportune to suggest that a similar practice existed in the nineteenth century. A similar situation arises with regard to the flageolet. Recorder players (especially amateurs) both in the past and in the present have sought to expand their instrument's somewhat limited repertoire by making appropriate arrangements of music intended for other instruments. Many arrangements of both csakan and flageolet music are currently in print and available to recorder players, ranging from solo works (some demanding considerable virtuosity) to concerti: examples include Heberle's concerto for csakan and his *Sonate Brilliante* for solo csakan, Krähmer's *Souvenir à la Suisse pour le Csakan seul*, and Bousquet's *Grandes Caprices pour Flageolet ou Flûte* of 1864.

## BRIDGE

The first work to be written for recorders in the course of the revival of the instrument appears to be a brief quartet composed by J.C.Bridge in order to demonstrate the 'Chester' recorders of Bressan at a lecture recital in 1901. The piece is a mere 62 bars long and is scored for alto, voice flute, tenor and basset recorders with the parts for the lower three instruments being confined to the lower octave of the instruments: the first part (for an alto recorder in f') requires a compass of a ninth. A short extract appears as Example II.

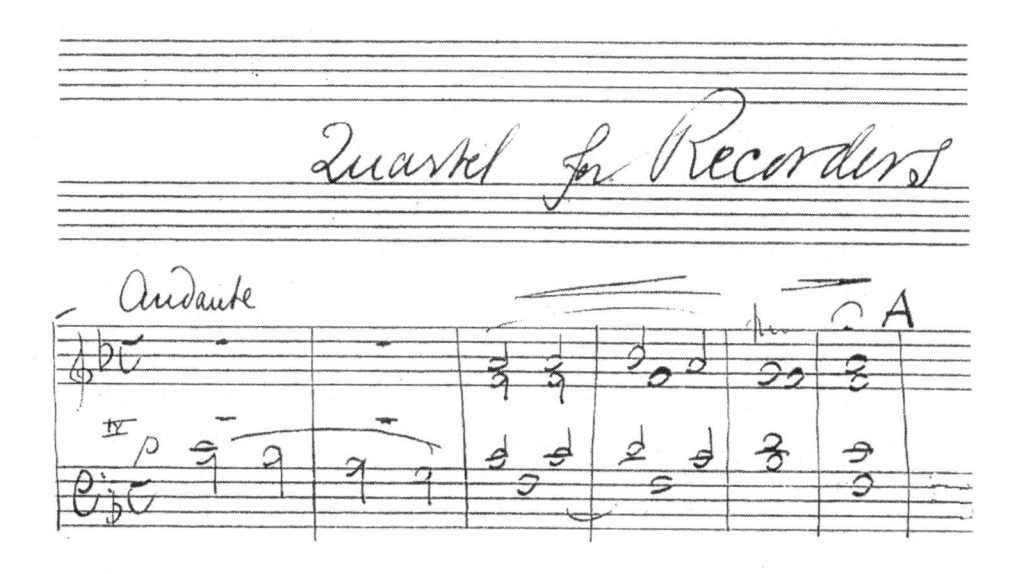

Example II

Bridge: quartet for recorders

Reproduced by permission of Chester and Cheshire Archives
(ZCR 62/2/83)

## TREATISES

Many treatises ('self-tutors') for the recorder survive from the eighteenth century, but only a handful from the nineteenth; they were published to cater for the needs of the amateur market. The English treatises fall into two categories, those for the recorder alone (for example, *Compleat Instructions for the Common Flute* published by Longman and Broderip in 1780) and the so-called 'universal tutors' which contained instructions for several instruments, often including the recorder. The *Muses Delight* published by Sadler in Liverpool in 1754 is a typical example: it contains instructions for the voice, violin, harpsichord or spinnet [sic], German flute, common flute, hautboy, French horn, bassoon and bass-violin. Both types of treatise include instruction on technique, rudiments of music, fingering charts, scales and tunes to play. The tunes are usually those which were in popular memory at the time of writing and often included folk songs and operatic

## The Recorder In The Nineteenth Century

arias: the standard of playing which could be achieved using such a treatise alone would not (to put it mildly) have been high, but it is of interest that one of Arnold Dolmetsch's early forays into the recorder world occurred when he studied the instrument from *The Compleat Flute-Master* of 1695 whilst on a voyage to America in 1905.

As the recorder declined in popularity the supply of treatises waned. Warner cited 246 treatises published between 1800 and 1830: of these, 86 are for the (transverse) flute, 53 for the flageolet, three for the csakan yet only one for the recorder.[61] Although Warner's work is now over 40 years old, it still provides an overview of the position with regard to the popularity of various instruments. Two further treatises have subsequently come to light.

Warner cites the treatise of Swain (1818):

THE YOUNG MUSICIAN/or the/Science of Music/familiarly explained:/with a glossary/of musical terms, and phrases by N.Swaine.

The volume was published in Stourport, England and a copy is located in the British Library (BL 1042.e.32). The preface to the section on the recorder begins:

Of wind instruments, the English Flute is the most simple and pleasing. It is also properest for children because a fife or German Flute is more injurious to the lungs...after the instrument is procured it will be necessary neatly to plug up the thumb or under hole, leaving a small opening to one side. It has been customary to apply the nail when some of the highest notes were required which could not be done with facility. It is proposed that the thumb be slided [sic] on and off the small opening, rather than putting the nail across.

It should be noted that it would be impossible to achieve accurate intonation – or even comfortable sounding – of the high notes with this technique. The process of 'thumbing' or 'pinching' is critical when playing in the higher register of the instrument and is frequently a cause of difficulty for the inexperienced player.

The treatise also covers the piano, voice, German flute and flageolet: fingering charts are given for both recorder and flageolet. Higbee has shed doubt on the notion that the English flute and recorder were one and the same instrument, but examination of the text suggests that Swaine was indeed referring to the recorder, often at that period referred to as the English flute. Although the fingerings given are not those in current use (modern 'baroque' fingering) there is no doubt that they are distinct from those given for the flageolet.

---

61  Warner, T.E., 'Indications of Performance Practice in Woodwind Instruction Books of the seventeenth and eighteenth Centuries', PhD diss., New York University, 1964

Another late treatise (although essentially a reprint of an older publication) was by William Tans'ur:

The Elements of Music made Easy; or, An Universal Introduction to the whole of music, etc.

The volume was published under that title in 1767 although it was essentially a new edition of 'A New Musical Grammar' dating from 1746. A late edition was published around 1820: a copy is held in the British Library (1509/1041) but the title page bearing the date of publication is missing. As the title implies, this is a universal tutor containing both the theory of music and practical instruction for a number of instruments, including the recorder which is here given its early eighteenth century English appellation 'flute'. Chapter III, headed 'Of the Common FLUTE or FLAGELET [sic] begins;

The flute is a *pipe,* a *wind-instrument,* and blown by the mouth: having eight holes; seven on top for the *fingers,* and one underneath for the *Thumb* of the Left Hand; which *Tones* are changed by *stopping* and *opening* the Holes, placing your 3 first fingers of your *Left Hand* uppermost, towards your mouth; and the 4 Fingers of your *Right Hand* towards the Bottom, and blowing at the same time, you'll have a production of the *Sound..* [italics and capitals original]

The author then illustrates the fingering for the diatonic scale of F major before discussing the second octave ('pinched' notes) and chromatic fingerings. He indicates that there are many sizes of flutes but all may be played by the 'foregoing rules'.

Three points are worthy of comment. Firstly, it is clear that the 'left hand uppermost' technique was standard at the time, whereas in former days some players would have preferred to play with the right hand uppermost. Secondly, the fingerings given differ only in small detail from current 'baroque' fingering and, thirdly, Tans'ur often leaves a finger of the right hand on the instrument even when not required for intonation. This is an early example of the buttress (or *Stützfinger*) technique wherein the fourth finger of the right hand is placed on the foot-joint to steady the recorder.

Although it is tempting to consider the existence of this treatise as evidence for the continued use of the recorder, it may equally be argued that the publisher did not wish to make substantial alterations to a publication which had been in existence for over half a century.

Johann Joseph Klein's *Lehrbuch der theoretischen Musik in systematischer Ordnung* (Systematic Textbook of Musical Theory) was published by W.Heinsius in Leipzig and Gera in 1801, and, like Tans'ur's method, reprinted material from an earlier publication. Klein discusses five sizes of recorder (in C and F) and notes that the recorder is also known as *die Flaute douce* (soft flute) or quiet flute (*stille Flöte*) and comments that the instrument uses less air than other wind instruments and that children can learn it

## The Recorder In The Nineteenth Century

without danger to their health. This observation is paralleled in Swain's treatise. Klein also describes the French flageolet with four or six finger-holes and two thumb-holes. I am indebted to Dr. Albert Rice for drawing my attention to this publication.[62]

Two universal tutors purporting to give instruction for many instruments were published in the first twenty years of the nineteenth century, but neither of these include a method for the recorder. Gehot's 'Complete Instructions for every Musical Instrument' of 1801 gives 'the Scale or Gamut' for thirty-five instruments (but not the recorder) and Goodale's 'The Instrumental Director, containing Rules for all Musical Instruments in Common Use' of 1819 again makes no reference to the recorder. One may conclude that the market for recorder tutors was largely a matter of history by the early nineteenth century.

## THE USE OF THE RECORDER

In the apparent absence of a repertoire, it is appropriate to investigate the use to which the few extant recorders were (or might have been) put, and a search of the literature revealed isolated examples of recorders being played in the nineteenth century. Several performances during the early days of the recorder revival (1885-1905) are discussed in the chapter dealing with the revival, but some isolated instances (and speculations) are related below.

## CHURCH MUSIC

The omnipresence of the organ in English churches dates from the latter years of the nineteenth century: many organs were destroyed at the Reformation, few parishes were wealthy enough in the early nineteenth century to replace the instruments, and the overall standard of liturgy (in the Church of England at least) was poor. Music was provided by church bands located in the west gallery of the church, these bands being composed mainly of amateur players – no doubt of very mixed ability – and musical arrangements varied according to the availability of both players and instruments. Had recorders been available, it is likely that they would have been used, but MacDermott (writing in 1948) found no evidence to support this hypothesis although he noted the use of the flute, fife, transverse flageolet [sic] and tin whistle.[63] In a personal communication, Sally Drage advised me of the use of a recorder in a church in Shipley, Kent (UK) which was used by the Parish Clerk to give the pitch for unaccompanied singing.[64] The recorder in question

---

62   Rice, A.R., personal communication, May 2007
63   MacDermott, K.H., *The Old Church Gallery Minstrels*, (London: SPCK 1948), p22
64   Drage, S., personal communication, 2005

is an alto by William or Robert Cotton (c1707-1775, c1735-p1794) and is currently located in the Tunbridge Wells museum.

There is evidence that the recorder was used in church services in Switzerland, which until the twentieth century did not enjoy its present prosperity. In Reformed cantons organs were forbidden but in other theological traditions (Roman Catholic) they were permitted although there was often little money for their purchase and wind instruments were used to accompany the psalms. The alto recorders by Löhner (N25, 26, now in the Historisches Museum, Basel) were used to accompany services at Adelboden.[65]

A footnote in Degen's *Zur Geschichte der Blockflöte in den germanishen Ländern* suggests a late use of the recorder in Flanders.[66] In 1855 two *Grossflöten* (large flutes) were discovered: these instruments were at one time played in the St. Lawrence market in the town of Eenaeme and older people recalled hearing a quartet of the instruments being played on quiet evenings in the Benedictine abbey. The recorders were thought to be of seventeenth century Flemish manufacture and eventually passed into the hands of the Belgian collector Caesar Snoeck.

## SECULAR USE

There are no references to the recorder being used in folk music, but Corcoran tells of the use of a recorder by Steenbergen (1676-1752):

> The instrument belonged to his [Harold Coates] grandfather, Thomas Davies, of Halkwin, Flintshire, who was born in 1830 and played it from his boyhood days throughout his life: Mr Coates himself remembers him playing it in 1914. It seems to me that at any rate one recorder was being played during the period of musical history when we thought it was silenced.[67]

On the other side of the Atlantic Ocean, 'English Flutes' (presumably recorders) were advertised for sale in the *New England Palladium* of October 27 1815.[68] It has been suggested that recorders were used in marching bands in the American Civil War of 1861-1865: this proposition requires further examination, for a more widespread use of the instrument away from the European mainland would be of considerable interest.

Waitzman, in his article 'The Decline of the Recorder in the eighteenth Century' of 1967 suggests that the recorder was used as a marching band instrument in the Civil War,

---

[65] Nef, K., *Musikinstrumenten Katalog Historisches Museum, Basel*, (Basel: Birkhauser 1906), p12
[66] Degen, D., *Zur Geschichte der Blockflöte in den germanishen Ländern*, (Kassel: Bärenreiter 1939), fn271, p139
[67] Corcoran, R.E., 'Did the Recorder really die out in England', *Recorder and Music Magazine*, 1/9, (1965), p2
[68] Music, D.W., 'The Recorder in early America', *The American Recorder* XXIV/3, (1983), pp102-103

*The Recorder In The Nineteenth Century*

taking as his source the comments of C.W.Brewster in his *Rambles about Portsmouth*:[69]

> For music, there are two drums for training days, while no less than fifteen hautboys and soft recorders are provided to cheer the immigrants in their solitude.

Bevan, in the *New Grove Dictionary of Musical Instruments* of 1984,[70] observes that the first known band to emerge in America was founded in 1635 and quotes the above text. A dichotomy is readily apparent when the opinion of Waitzman is compared with Bevan: the former suggests that recorders were used in the Civil War period, whereas the latter suggests that the citation refers to the seventeenth century. A critical reading of Brewster's text reveals that it is a chronology of the progressive colonization of New Hampshire beginning with the first visitor arriving at the shores of the Piscataqua river in 1603, and in an inventory of 1635 Brewster notes the existence of a great house, a manor and a sawmill: he talks of plantations and armaments, also writing that 'for music, there are two drums etc.'.

This text patently refers to the events of 1635 and not to the Civil War and that any reading of the text suggesting that recorders were played in the nineteenth century is erroneous: other texts relating to bands in the Civil War period fail to refer to recorders. Recorders (and flageolets – see below) are both soft instruments which would hardly be audible in a military band and unsuited to outdoor use. Even a moderate gust of wind across the window of a recorder will render the instrument mute – as may be demonstrated by playing out-of-doors on a windy day, or by the simple experiment of directing a hairdryer at the window of a recorder whilst it is being played.

It is however, likely that duct flutes were used in America in the mid-nineteenth century. An hybrid instrument is included in the present inventory (recorder D5) which was made by Firth and Pond of New York between 1856 and 1862: it possesses a sponge cap and one key below the lowest tone-hole. Some authors have described it as a recorder, although Kuronen considers the instrument to be a flageolet; its present location is not known. This instrument lends credence to the use of duct flutes at the time, but the evidence for their use in marching bands is far from compelling.

---

69   Brewster, C.W., *Rambles about Portsmouth*, (Portsmouth: N.H., C.W. Brewster Vol I 1859), p19
70   *The New Grove Dictionary of Musical Instruments*, ed Sadie, S., (London: Macmillan 1984) s.v. Bands (Bevan, C.)

## CONCLUSION

It must be conceded that there appears to have been little music composed for the recorder and little documented evidence for its use in the nineteenth century. The majority of extant instruments (with the exception of the Bavarian recorders) are altos, voice flutes and tenors, all of which could conceivably been used to play music written for the violin, flute, or oboe. It is likely that the few recorder players of the nineteenth century would have adapted and arranged music intended for other instruments to meet their particular needs, such practice being common amongst recorder players from the renaissance to the present day.

In short, it is still not possible to give a definitive answer to Dolmetsch's question 'and what was played on them?' Relatively few recorders existed in the nineteenth century and composers would have been reluctant to write for the instrument: perceptive speculation suggests that players made their own arrangements or learnt folk music by the age-old aural tradition.

# CHAPTER VII

## THE RECORDER IN ART AND LITERATURE

The visual and literary arts can provide the musicologist with pertinent information relating to familiarity with, and use of, a musical instrument and such secondary evidence may be of value in placing an instrument in its historical context.

### THE VISUAL ARTS

Musical instruments have been portrayed in visual art since the days of the great classical civilizations of ancient Greece and Rome. From the Middle Ages to the present day, artists have painted (and sculptors have carved) musical instruments in contexts ranging from the sacred to the secular, from portrait to landscape, from the precise depiction of instruments to stylized realizations. A scrutiny of paintings of musical instruments demonstrates that some artists seek to represent instruments in accurate detail whereas for others the instruments only relate to persons, places or artefacts connected with music. This latter group is of interest to the organologist only insofar as such works may point to the circumstances in which the instrument was used at a given time in history but it is the former which may yield useful technical information. Caution must therefore be exercised in transferring iconographic evidence to historical or organological fact.

These comments apply essentially to contemporary art, that is, painting depicting events around the lifetime of the painter, but many works of art are realizations of historical or classical scenes and any depiction of instruments in these works is liable to be conjectural. Other works may show fantastical instruments: the Pre-Raphaelite artists exhibit this tendency and it is important to realize (in the context of the nineteenth-century recorder) that the late Pre-Raphaelites were contemporaries of those musicians who were responsible for the early revival of historical instruments. For a work of art to be of value in the study of an instrument it must provide a sufficiently convincing illustration of the instrument: for example, a painting which illustrates a duct flute (possibly a recorder or possibly a csakan or flageolet) is of little value in the present study. Many paintings depict a 'flute' or 'pipe': some specify a recorder, whilst others clearly illustrate a recorder but do not describe it as such. Flageolets and csakans may appear on first glance to be recorders but critical examination may reveal otherwise and painters themselves may not be entirely clear which instrument they are illustrating. Caution must be applied to 'artistic licence'!

The aim of the present chapter is less to present a comprehensive catalogue of works depicting the recorder in the nineteenth century than to capture a flavour of the

## The Recorder In The Nineteenth Century

awareness of the recorder by artists across Europe in that century. The principal source of reference used was Lander's website 'Recorder Iconography'[71] but reference was also made to the websites of RIDiM (Répertoire International d'Iconographie Musicale) and RCMI (Research Center for Musical Iconography), the Bridgeman Art Library and to an online search for photographs in the Lebrecht Musical Collection.

## THE WORKS OF ART

A brief description of some images displaying the recorder is given below. The author has been able to visualize reproductions of some of the paintings and can vouch for their verisimilitude, but in other cases the description given by other authors (notably the authoritative Anthony Rowland-Jones) has been taken as definitive.

1   The Shepherd Piper           Anderson, Sophie           1881           GB

   A young boy sits on a hillside playing a crudely-made recorder: the pastoral image of the instrument is well-attested in eighteenth century music.

2   The Rehearsal                Baumgartner, Peter         1834-1911      D

   The instruments include violin, flute, horn, double bass and a small recorder played by a young boy.

3   Les Aveugles                 Boilly, Louis-Léopold      1825           F

   Lithograph by François de Delpech after Boilly. Two street musicians, one playing the violin and singing, the other a duct flute which has the head of a recorder but a key above the first tone-hole, the key-flap extending to the head joint. A small boy holds out a tattered cap.

4   The Piping Shepherd          Fripp, Alfred Downing 1822-1845   GB

   On a chalk cliff before a lake a boy holds a small recorder as if to play it.

---

71  Lander N.S., Recorder Iconography, http://www.recorderhomepage.net/art.html

5   The Power of Music        Good, Thomas            1789-1872    GB
An old man dances to the music of a woman playing the 'cello and a young man playing a recorder.

6   The Shepherd Boy          Linnell, John           1831         GB
A young shepherd wearing a smock plays a baroque-style recorder while his sheep graze behind him and his dog stands beside him.

Shepherd boy (John Linnell)
Reproduce by permission of The Bridgeman Art Library, London

| | | | | |
|---|---|---|---|---|
| 7 | A Grand Review | Livesay, Richard | 1800 | GB |

A review of troops at Hatfield House, England: a young lad holds a baroque recorder of alto size.

| | | | | |
|---|---|---|---|---|
| 8 | St. Cecilia and Musical Angels | Nadorp, Franz | 1794-1836 | D |

On a bench beneath the figure lie a lute, a violin and bow, and a tambourine, beneath which is a partially-hidden recorder.

| | | | | |
|---|---|---|---|---|
| 9 | The Violinist Jean-Joseph Bott as a Child | Anonymous | c1836 | D |

The violinist plays but a recorder lies in front of him on music for two violins by Louis Spohr (1784-1859).

| | | | | |
|---|---|---|---|---|
| 10 | Façade Decorations | Cassone, Francesco | c1842 | I |

Ten recorders are shown on the façade of the Teatro Vittorio Emmanuele II, Noto, Sicily

| | | | | |
|---|---|---|---|---|
| 11 | Decorated Piano | Gamble, John | c1870 | GB |

The piano case is decorated with a painted design depicting Apollo with his lyre and various musical instruments, including a renaissance-style bass recorder (303-1882) from the museum's collection (Victoria and Albert Museum, London: 11-1913).

| | | | | |
|---|---|---|---|---|
| 12 | Drawing from Scrapbook | Faraday, Michael | 1791-1867 | GB |

The sketch by the physicist shows a recorder with a straight horn together with a triangle.

| | | | | |
|---|---|---|---|---|
| 13 | Manet's daughter playing the Recorder | Morisot, Berthe | 1841-1895 | F |

A colour pencil drawing of a young girl playing a recorder.

The Pre-Raphaelites (and their successors the Aesthetic Movement and the Arts and Crafts Movement) might be expected to have depicted recorders and other instruments, given their interest in recapturing the spirit of late mediaeval artists whose paintings often (and often accurately) depicted instruments. By the late nineteenth century (when these artistic movements were in full flood) the early music revival had begun: indeed, the founder of the Arts and Crafts Movement, William Morris, was acquainted with Arnold Dolmetsch. The instruments appearing in Pre-Raphaelite Art (both early and late) seldom bear substantial resemblance to classical instruments, and are more often stylized fanciful creations.

The works cited above, however, are a representative example of what transpires to be a surprisingly large canvas. They are distributed across Europe and throughout the century, demonstrating an awareness of the recorder rather greater than would be anticipated from the widely-held perception of its virtual disappearance from the late eighteenth century onwards. It is not clear how many of these artists actually saw (or, less probably, heard) a recorder but they certainly possessed an awareness of its outward appearance.

## PHOTOGRAPHS

No photographs of the recorder in the very early days of its revival have hitherto come to light.

*The Recorder In The Nineteenth Century*

## LITERATURE

In contrast to the visual arts, there are few references to the recorder, at least in the English literature: a number of references to musical dictionaries are cited in relevant parts of the present text, but a search of Lander's website 'Theatrical and Literary References to the Recorder' revealed few entries.[72] The site only encompasses English literature; no comparable source of French and German literature is known to the present author, but nevertheless a few quotations of interest in the history of the recorder are given below.

Charles Dickens refers to the recorder in his *Great Expectations* (1861) when Pip and his companions attend a performance of Shakespeare's *Hamlet,* a play which makes explicit reference to the recorder. Of rather greater interest is Sir Richard Burton's *The Book of the Thousand Nights and a Night* (1885-1888). Burton was an English traveller and writer who translated the *Kama Sutra* and *The Arabian Nights* into English, and his *The Book of a Thousand Nights* he describes a Middle Eastern meal:

> At last they brought out a fine wine service with rich old wine, and we sat down to drink and sing some songs and others played the lute and psaltery and recorders and other instruments, and the bowl went merrily around.

It is surprising that Burton was familiar with the recorder in the 1880s. Recorders were first heard in London in 1885 and some thirteen years had to elapse before Christopher Welch was to give his lecture on 'Literature relating to the Recorder' to The Musical Association.

In her book *Der Csakan und seine Musik* (p47) Betz notes that the important German romantic author Johann Wolfgang von Goethe (1749-1832) in his *Novelle* of 1828 makes reference to a soft sweet flute with a short beak which possessed a charming tone and in his *Dichtung und Wahrheit* (Fact and Fantasy) mentions *einer Flûte-douce* which is most probably a recorder. Betz also quotes Jean Paul (a *nom de plume* of Johann Paul Friedrich Richter [1763-1825]) who described a rather unseemly brawl between a bass player and a *Flüte-a-beccist* [sic] in his *Flegeljahr* (Adolescence) of 1804.

Painters appear to have been more aware of the recorder than writers: perhaps they saw the value of the recorder in certain styles of painting (such as pastoral scenes) whereas writers placed less emphasis on such nebulous concepts, but nevertheless both artists and men of letters provide evidence for an awareness of the recorder either as an historical or freshly rediscovered entity.

---

72  Lander, N.S., Literary and theatrical References to the Recorder http://www.recorderhomepage.net/quotes.html

# CHAPTER VIII

## INTRODUCTION TO THE RECORDER REVIVAL

Few events in history appear spontaneously as isolated phenomena, most being the product of a series of factors which interact to give birth to changes in thought and practice. Few events are the product of one person acting in isolation at a specific moment in time: trends are often apparent which not only transcend national boundaries but also occur over a number of years. Little was known of the recorder before the final quarter of the nineteenth century, but by the end of that century pioneers were collecting, restoring, playing and making recorders. The recorder revival can only be contextualized as being a product of the whole early music movement and in order to place the recorder revival in context it is necessary to examine the history of, and the reasons for, the early music movement – as indeed it was appropriate to study the reasons for the recorder's decline in the late eighteenth century.

## THE GENESIS OF THE EARLY MUSIC MOVEMENT

The early music movement is a well-recognized phenomenon in twenty-first century musical life and it is through the activities of that movement that the recorder was revived, first by a small number of enthusiasts, subsequently leading to the instrument gradually making its way into mainstream musical practice. Its rediscovery and development are inextricably linked with the revival of other early instruments and their music and, indeed, an interest in music of former times may be traced back many hundreds of years although a widespread interest in such music is of relatively recent origin. The term 'early music movement' conjures up a vision of musicians playing in an unconventional style (what, one may rightly ask, is convention?) and upon unconventional instruments but which may be better described as an interest in, and an involvement with, music of the past. Such a description places the early music movement in a cognate environment of musicology, organology, performance practice and sociology.

The early music movement may be traced back to the early years of the nineteenth century (albeit with roots in earlier periods) although widespread activity in the field only occurred in the closing years of that century. History abounds in movements and their associated counter-movements (the Protestant Reformation and the Catholic Counter-Reformation being outstanding examples) and also in episodes of massive social change which alter the course of people and nations, these events often coming about as a reaction against a particular set of circumstances (of which the French Revolution is typical). Two movements in the nineteenth century appear to be of relevance in the early music revival: although one was artistic and the other sociological, both led to reactions and counter-reactions. Romanticism pervaded the arts throughout the nineteenth century, and industrialization changed the face of society, particularly in England.

## ROMANTICISM

In discussing the revival of early music and the recorder it is appropriate to give brief consideration to the topic of romanticism, perhaps the most significant movement to impact on the arts in the nineteenth century. Romanticism followed hard upon the heels of classicism: during the classical period the recorder declined in importance and during the age of romanticism it lay largely un-noticed in the overall spectrum of music. The decline of romanticism in the late nineteenth century heralded new trends in musical culture, one of these being the revival of early music – and, with it, the recorder

Romanticism – arising in the 1770s – reacted against order and rationality, against the cool logic of the intellect which pervaded classicism, and in its place favoured a more individual, spontaneous and emotional outpouring from the artist or composer. Its origin lay partly in the folk arts (expressing the voice of the people over and against the ruling aristocracy) and politically it may be aligned with the French Revolution. Romanticism tended to create a desire to return to – and exalt – a perceived ideal world which had been long lost and during the course of the nineteenth century many artists of the romantic school demonstrated an affection for the mediaeval and gothic arts with their powerful heroes and heroines. The romantic ideal of re-creating an idealized past was, in reality, doomed to failure as art and humanity inevitably evolve: the desire to re-create the historical past is, in itself, a relatively modern phenomenon which must be viewed with a degree of critical scepticism, for the past can only be envisaged in terms of the present. In passing, it should be noted that, at the time of writing (2007), the quest for 'authenticity' in musical performance so characteristic of the early music movement of the 1970s and 1980s has undergone a paradigm shift and is now spoken of as 'historically informed performance practice'. The apotheosis of authenticity has been replaced by a rigorous academic process which is better able to contextualize the present in terms of the past.

The formality of the classical period was to give way to a period wherein emotion triumphed over reason, sense and feeling over intellect. The romantics (whether musicians, artists or men of letters) rejoiced in the spontaneous expression of feeling, in particular in matters of love and romance: the artist himself (very rarely herself) became a purveyor of emotion rather than a paid servant who produced works of art to the order of an aristocratic patron. Social factors – in terms of a developing plutocracy related to industrialization, a rise in a relatively wealthy middle class and a diminishing number of aristocratic courts – led to an isolation of the romantic artist within society. Art was ceasing to be the privilege of a few wealthy patrons.

## Introduction To The Recorder Revival

In music, the romantic era essentially began with Beethoven (1770-1827) although some commentators consider him to be the last classical rather than the first romantic composer. The full flood of romanticism, however, is heard in the works of such composers as Schumann, Chopin, Liszt, Brahms and Wagner but, by the end of the nineteenth century, romanticism had essentially run its course in music having bequeathed to the world a plethora of music which remains in the popular repertoire over one hundred years later. Out of the romantic tradition were born significant new styles of music including neo-romanticism (R.Strauss, Mahler, Elgar), impressionism (Debussy) and neo-classicism (Stravinsky, Les Six): as romanticism gave way to these new styles, yet another movement was beginning to flower. It is known to us as the early music movement.

On the subject of romanticism, Fubini makes a fascinatingly perceptive comment relating to the revival of early music:

> ...we should note that the early and middle years of the nineteenth century were at one and the same time both revolutionary and backward-looking, both fascinated by the abstraction, the rigour, and the religious qualities of the great church music of the sixteenth century and preoccupied with the creation of new forms expressly at odds with a tradition that no longer seemed to have a relevant yardstick to offer contemporary composers.[75]

There is much to show for Fubini's 'nostalgic backward glance'. Throughout the nineteenth century early music was being discovered and played, beginning with renaissance polyphony and (particularly in Germany) the great choral works of J.S Bach. In painting, the Pre-Raphaelites were heavily influenced by mediaeval and renaissance art: the plays of Shakespeare were enjoying a new-found popularity, and architects turned once more to the gothic for inspiration.

Parallel to this discovery – which gained in momentum as the nineteenth century progressed – there appeared (in music at least) a reaction to the grand scale of the romantic symphony and opera in the form of a renaissance of the delicate tapestry of early vocal, keyboard, and string music.

Many movements throughout history (in art, in science, in politics, in theology) lead on to fresh ideas: as romanticism arose out of classicism, impressionism arose out of romanticism. Other movements lead to a counter-reaction, a retrogression to former ideas and ideals. Herein lie at least some of the seeds of the genesis of the early music movement.

---

[75] Fubini, E., *A History of Musical Aesthetics*, trans. Hatwell, M., (London: Macmillan 1991), p180

## THE INDUSTRIAL REVOLUTION

It may seem improbable – certainly in comparison with romanticism – that the Industrial Revolution should have an influence upon music but it must be recalled that the arts not only express the feelings of the individual artist but also the collective contemporary ethos. Access to the arts is facilitated – or limited – by finance, leisure time, accessibility and transport amongst other things. Small aristocratic courts were becoming a thing of the past in the nineteenth century, whereas new theatres, concerts halls and galleries were being opened and travel facilitated. More and more people lived in towns and had sufficient wealth not only to visit artistic events but also to give financial support to such ventures; many of these changes relate to the social impact of the Industrial Revolution.

Massive change swept over European (and especially English) lifestyle in the period c1750 to 1900 and, as industry superseded country life and agriculture, town life became the norm over and against a pastoral country background, whilst mechanization and industrialization changed the face of society. Workmen were forced to work intolerable hours often under dangerous conditions for appallingly low wages and it is hardly surprising that a two-tier society came into being – in the words of Karl Marx, the bourgeoisie and the proletariat. The proletariat often lived under conditions of grinding poverty whilst the rich factory owners lived in comfort and had an increasing opportunity to follow and to finance artistic endeavour.

Social and political changes have often exerted an influence upon the arts and to almost any movement there is almost always a reaction (as has been shown in respect of romanticism). In the decorative arts, the work of William Morris (England) in the late nineteenth century was perceived to be a reaction against industrialization, for Morris sought to counter the effects of mass production in the factory by encouraging individual craftsmanship. Pugin, in the field of architecture, sought to restore the elegance of the high gothic over the black factories and chimneys of the Industrial Revolution. I believe that it is reasonable to speculate that part of the enthusiasm for early music – even if but only a small part of that enthusiasm – is related to rejection of, and retaliation against, the massive depersonalizing forces of industrialization with its 'dark satanic mills'. The return to the elegant simplicity of the music of former years may have, amongst its roots, rather more than just a reaction against romanticism and its huge orchestras.

There may well be other strands which contributing to the early music revival but which cannot be precisely identified, but two factors – drawn from the arts – are of relevance in facilitating the study of early music and its instruments.

## MUSICOLOGY AND INSTRUMENT COLLECTIONS

The science of musicology dates from the mid-nineteenth century. As interest in the music of former times developed, scholars began to unearth long-forgotten works from libraries and accord them critical study: it must be recalled that, before the revival of interest in early music, nearly all the music performed in concert halls, opera houses and (to a lesser extent) the church was of contemporary origin.

The first attempts at performing early music used modern instruments (in Mendelssohn's pioneering performance of the St. Matthew Passion at Leipzig in 1829 the oboe d'amore parts were played on clarinets) but later in the nineteenth century musicians began to take old instruments out of their glass cases in museums and restore them to playing condition, the process facilitated by the increasing obsession with the collection of artefacts, a pan-European phenomenon of the age: long-forgotten instrumental techniques were re-learnt, often from surviving treatises. The tools required for the revival of early music and its appropriate instruments were becoming available. The eminent organologist Curt Sachs, as early as 1942, wrote:

> The reconstruction of ancient instruments as well as critical editions of Complete Works were symbolic of a growing interest in music of remote epochs. Also originally an outgrowth of the romantic period, the historical movement in music became a leading force in neutralizing the excesses of the later romantic styles, such as decomposition of form, its obliteration of distinct outlines, its harmonic and colloristic [sic] super-refinement, its calculated effect on the listener, its added subjectivity.[74]

It is not possible to pinpoint one definitive catalyst which precipitated the early music revival, for many factors interacted to bring about an enthusiasm for the musical past at a time when travel and communication were becoming easier. Several salient factors have been outlined, but it is also relevant to note that the late nineteenth century produced a number of scholarly musicians who made the rediscovery of ancient music their life's work.

## A BRIEF SYNOPSIS OF THE HISTORY OF THE EARLY MUSIC MOVEMENT

Many consider that the early music movement began with Mendelssohn's 1829 performance of Bach's *St. Matthew Passion* but there is substantial evidence that an interest in music of former times existed long before this date. Even in mediaeval times

---

[74] Sachs, C., *The History of Musical Instruments*, (London: J.M.Dent & Sons Ltd. 1942), p450

troubadour music was committed to paper long after the death of the composer/performer and in the sixteenth century some groups (notably the Sistine Chapel Choir) performed music written fifty or more years previously: it should be remembered that this was an epoch when only contemporary music was fashionable and frequently performed. In the 1720s Pepusch's London Academy of Ancient Music was performing renaissance choral music and the massive Handel Commemoration Festival of 1784 (with 525 singers and players!) attracted widespread attention to that composer's music; as the eighteenth century gave way to the nineteenth a process of rediscovery of old music was blossoming across the continent of Europe.

In Germany attention focused on the great choral works of J.S.Bach and by 1850 the Bach Gesellschaft editions were available: the first performance of a baroque opera (Handel's *Almira*) was given at Hamburg in 1876. In Vienna, the activities of Baron von Swieten and Raphael Georg Keisewetter established a fashionable taste for music of the renaissance and baroque. Considerable interest in both choral and instrumental music was apparent in Paris, Alexandre Choron establishing a school of classical and religious music in 1816 which became La Sociètè de Musique Vocale et Classique in 1841, whilst in the religious sphere Dom Prosper Guéranger OSB, Monk of Solesmes, began his researches into plainchant in the 1840s. François-Joseph Fétis initiated his historical concerts in Paris using lute, viols and harpsichord in 1832 and by 1860 Louis Diémer was given harpsichord recitals: he established La Sociètè des Instruments Anciens in 1890. Fétis continued his performances of early music on moving to Brussels and in the 1870s Victor-Charles Mahillon became the first curator of the instrumental collection in that city. In the Conservatoire attempts were made to play early instruments, one of these performances being witnessed by the young Arnold Dolmetsch (see chapter IX).

In London, historical instruments (including recorders) appeared in the International Inventions Exhibition of 1885, the musicologist A.J.Hipkins gave a recital on historic keyboard instruments at the annual conference of the Incorporated Society of Musicians in 1893 and, around the same time, Arnold Dolmetsch began to give recitals of early music in his house at Dulwich. In the field of vocal music Richard Terry (appointed to Westminster Cathedral in 1901) encouraged an interest in performing music of the renaissance whilst Francis William Galpin explored early instruments.

These brief notes serve to highlight the fact that the early music movement was a pan–European phenomenon, embraced by many scholarly musicians: for a more detailed history of the genesis of the early music movement, the reader is referred to Haskell's *The Early Music Revival – a History*.[75] It is only in the final years of the nineteenth century that the first signs of the recorder revival may be discerned but it should be recalled that the recorder has never been a major player on the stage of European art music, taking second place to the transverse flute and oboe. It revival appears to have

---

75  Haskell, H., *The Early Music Revival – a History*, (London: Thames and Hudson Ltd., 1988)

begun almost simultaneously in four European countries – England, France, Germany and Belgium.

*The Recorder In The Nineteenth Century*

# CHAPTER IX

## THE REVIVAL OF THE RECORDER

### ENGLAND

The revival of the recorder in England is a story of people, of exhibitions, of lectures, and of sporadic performances, the latter often given to illustrate lectures. The revival of an old instrument is integrally related to that of the overall revival of early music and in England one man stood head and shoulders above all others. His name was Arnold Dolmetsch. Although Dolmetsch's role in the early revival of the recorder is minimal, his life's work was devoted to early music and he was without any doubt a seminal figure in the early music movement.

### ARNOLD DOLMETSCH

The very name 'Dolmetsch' evokes a picture of the early music revival in general and of the recorder in particular, for it is widely believed that Arnold Dolmetsch was substantially responsible for the revival of the recorder and that this work was continued by his son, Carl. That Arnold Dolmetsch played a role in the history of the recorder cannot be denied, but it is necessary to place his work in an accurate historical context.

Eugène Arnold Dolmetsch was born on 24th. February 1858 in the town of Le Mans, France. As a child he received tuition on the piano and on the violin, subsequently studying the latter instrument with the celebrated player Henri Vieuxtemps in Brussels, where he enrolled in the Conservatoire in 1879. Towards the close of that year he was present at a *Concert historique* where he heard for the first time music of the late baroque played upon harpsichord, virginals, positif organ and viols. Whilst being impressed with the sound of the music Dolmetsch remembered sensing that 'something was not quite right'. It was in Brussels, also, that Dolmetsch first heard recorders, for one of the professors determined to give a lecture on early wind instruments. Margaret Campbell, authoress of the definitive biography of Arnold Dolmetsch, describes the occasion:

> A number of students were chosen to demonstrate and when they came to the early recorders the professor allotted them to the instrumentalists who were, in his opinion, playing the modern equivalent. The bassoonist was given the bass recorder, the clarinettist the tenor, and the flute and piccolo players the treble and descant... Derisive laughter greeted every attempt and one student remarked that he could not understand our forebears using such dreadful instruments. 'How

could they be so un-musical?' he asked. But Dolmetsch was not at all satisfied at this total rejection of the instruments, and thereby in a sense also the music, of a bygone age: he remembered thinking that we do not dismiss the painters and writers of the same period merely because their style is not identical to our own.[76]

At this time the Conservatoire at Brussels lay at the hub of the discovery and restoration of old instruments.

In 1883 Dolmetsch crossed the English Channel to commence eighteen months' study at the newly opened Royal College of Music in London and began to study the music of Purcell and earlier composers in the college library. In 1890 he purchased his first 'ancient instrument' (a viola d'amore by Testore) and throughout the 1890s his work of discovering, editing, and performing early music was gathering pace. Dolmetsch had been trained as an instrument maker and was now able to restore both keyboard and stringed instruments (the latter mainly being viols). His services were occasionally required to illustrate lectures and to provide music for Shakespearean performances but it is important to indicate that Dolmetsch was essentially a string and keyboard instrument player, Campbell noting that apart from hearing recorders in Brussels, he had not experimented with early wind instruments. In 1892 he visited Chester to assist Dr. J.C.Bridge in a series of three lectures on *Music of the Past*, playing (with his daughter Hélène) on viol, lute, and spinet to illustrate the third lecture *The Early Instrumental Writers of England*. The 'Chester' recorders (see below, 'J.C.Bridge') were demonstrated at the first lecture but Dolmetsch does not appear to have come into contact with the instruments although doubtless he would have seen the programme.

In the mid 1890s Dolmetsch provided music for a number of Shakespeare plays produced by William Poel: his players dressed in period costume and played upon period instruments, Dolmetsch himself playing pipe and tabor in a performance of *The Tempest* in 1897.

It is widely held that Dolmetsch did not play the recorder until he purchased an alto recorder by Peter Bressan (1663-1731) in 1905, but recent research by Alexandra Williams in the Dolmetsch family archive at Haslemere suggests that this supposition is incorrect.[77] Dolmetsch appears to have played the recorder in public two occasions in 1900, the first being during a performance of Shakespeare's *Hamlet* given by the Elizabethan Stage Society (directed by Poel) on 21st. February, the second being at a meeting of the same society on 11th. March. The programme note for *Hamlet* (illustrated in Williams' thesis) lists the use of 'Three viols, a Lute, a Recorder, an Oboe, Trumpets and Drum', Dolmetsch himself playing viols, lute, and recorder, with Beatrice Horne playing the oboe and

---

76  Campbell, M., *Dolmetsch: the Man and his Work*, (London: Hamish Hamilton 1975), p12
77  Williams, A., 'The Dodo was really a Phoenix: the Renaissance and Revival of the Recorder in England 1879-1941', unpublished PhD diss., University of Melbourne, (2005), pp74-75

Dolmetsch's first wife, Elodie, playing the trumpet.[78] The March meeting featured 'The Musical Instruments used in Shakespeare's Plays: Lutes, Citherns [sic], Viols, Virginals, Recorder, Trumpets, Sackbuts, Cornets, Hautboys'. Dolmetsch himself is listed as playing 'other instruments' – which would have included the last five named above as well as the viol and virginals.

Whereas there is no reason to doubt the veracity of these comments, they do pose two questions which require further discussion.

Firstly, there is no documentation describing the actual recorder which was played, and, secondly, it appears (as will be related below) that Dolmetsch only learnt the fingering of the instrument in 1905, the year he purchased his Bressan alto. His widow Mabel Dolmetsch's *Personal Recollections of Arnold Dolmetsch* suggests that Dolmetsch –as late as 1917- thought that he owned the only recorder in England, with the sole exception of the Chester recorders.[79] As an aside, it should be noted that this observation tends to confirm Dolmetsch's well-described isolation from the majority of the musical world! On the occasion of the loss of his Bressan recorder in 1919, Dolmetsch wrote of the loss of *le* recorder, but Campbell does suggest that he possessed two recorders at that time. In summary, it appears that Dolmetsch indeed played a recorder in 1900 but the tantalizing question of 'which recorder?' at present remains unanswered, although Williams speculates that he may have borrowed one of the Chester instruments: how well he played an instrument with whose fingering he was unfamiliar is also open to speculation and the eagerness with which he pursued the reproduction of the Bressan instrument after its loss in 1919 suggests that he perhaps possessed only this one recorder at the time.

Secondly, there arises the curious description of Dolmetsch playing a number of instruments with which he was not apparently familiar. Some fifteen years later he was to write:

Many of these [old woodwind instruments] have wholly disappeared – for example, the shawms, the cromornes, the cornets [cornett, zink], and the recorders:.. Only two amongst these lost instruments have yet been revived: the recorder and the 18th. century one-keyed flute. *The writer having no authority to speak of the others...*[80] [my italics- D.M.]

Dolmetsch was a fine violinist and a capable keyboard player but he seems to have had little enthusiasm for wind instruments and indeed his use of the Bressan recorder was confined to playing simple melodies in broken consorts rather than in exploring the

---

78  Williams, A., ibid., appendix 3, pp19-20
79  Dolmetsch, M., *Personal Recollections of Arnold Dolmetsch*, (London: Routledge and Keegan Paul 1957), p131
80  Dolmetsch, A., *The Interpretation of Music of the XVII and XVIII Centuries*, (London: Novello 1915), p457

sonata and concerto repertoire of the baroque. I incline to the view that, in the light of Dolmetsch's own comments, he probably demonstrated - and even sounded - the cornet, sackbut, and hautboy but he is unlikely to have played convincingly upon them.

In 1905 the violinist, harpsichordist, and lutenist made a purchase which has given rise to much erroneous thought about this great man of music, leading to the supposition that Dolmetsch was the prime mover in the recorder revival. He attended a sale of T.W. Taphouse' collection at Sotheby's on 7th. June 1905, his account of the event in his diary being related by Campbell:

Enfin, vers la fin j'ai acheté pour £2 un beau English recorder 1630 boxwood and ivory. Prefect preservation. Sweet tone…Cela me sera très utile.[81]

Campbell gives three extracts from Sotheby's catalogue of the day, including:

61. RECORDER or Flute à bec [sic], English, ivory, about 1730 *in leather case, a fine specimen.*
The buyer was Thompson and the price £5. 2s. 6d.

Campbell also suggests that there is no doubt that the recorder Dolmetsch bought was lot 61, and that '1630' must have been a slip of his pen.

An immediate disparity is revealed in this account of the purchase of the Bressan recorder: the Sotheby catalogue records the buyer as Thompson, and the purchase price £5. 2s. 0d, whereas Dolmetsch's diary (usually accurate) clearly states that he paid £2 for the instrument. More recent work by Meadows has shown that the item purchased by Dolmetsch was more probably lot 111 of the sale:[82]

111. VARIOUS. a box-wood and ivory recorder by Barton [sic]…

This information is compatible with Dolmetsch's diary and it would not be difficult (in the days when recorders and their makers were less familiar than today) for a clerk to confuse 'Barton' and 'Bressan'.

During a voyage to America late in 1905, Dolmetsch found an opportunity to learn to play his new instrument, for he had acquired a copy of *The Compleat Flute-Master or The whole Art of playing upon ye Rechorder* [sic], a recorder treatise dating from 1695, and, each evening as 'Minnehaha' crossed the Atlantic, Dolmetsch sat in his cabin acquiring a new skill as a recorder player. Dolmetsch's copy of *The Compleat Flute-Master* is preserved in the Dolmetsch Library at Haslemere, England, the recorder itself now being located

---

81 Campbell, M., Dolmetsch: the Man and his Work, p164
82 Meadows, H., 'Happy Birthday, whenever that may be', *The Recorder Magazine*, XV/3, (1995), pp87-88

## The Revival Of The Recorder

in the Dolmetsch Collection housed at the Horniman Museum in London. It therefore appears that Dolmetsch's skill on the recorder was essentially acquired in 1905, and this alone raises the question of his technical ability on the instrument in 1900.

Although the years beyond 1905 are strictly out of the context of the present study, a brief mention of the use of the recorder by Arnold Dolmetsch does not come amiss in order to place his work in its historical perspective. He began to introduce the recorder into his concerts, Mabel Dolmetsch observing:

> The introduction of the recorder appeared to us at the time in the light of an amusing novelty, bringing a new flavour to our concerts.[83]

The loss of the Bressan alto recorder by the young Carl Dolmetsch at Waterloo Station, London, in 1919 (one of the legends in the history of the revival of the instrument) caused his father Arnold to make his first recorder which, following much experimentation, he finished in 1920. A full consort of recorders played at the Haslemere Festival in 1926.

In connection with Dolmetsch's role in the revival of the recorder, O'Kelly writes:

> Because he is so much associated with the recorder, it is easy to forget – or fail to appreciate – that for many years the recorder occupied a peripheral role in Dolmetsch's music-making...It is interesting to speculate, indeed, whether Arnold Dolmetsch would ever have had the motivation to make a recorder at all had it not been for the irritating circumstances of the loss of his own Bressan alto fourteen years after he had bought it.[84]

Dolmetsch, although largely scorned by the musical establishment, was the leading figure in England in the rediscovery of early instrumental music at the turn of the nineteenth and twentieth centuries: his role in the recorder revival is further explored by the present author in *The Consort* 2007.[85] He was often difficult to deal with, being very self-opinionated (one reason why many of his significant peers ignored him) but his inexhaustible zeal as restorer, maker, player, and researcher of old music knew no bounds, and it would be not unreasonable to dub him the father of authenticity – certainly in England, and probably in the world.

---

83  Dolmetsch, M., *Personal Recollections of Arnold Dolmetsch*, p88
84  O'Kelly, E., 'The Recorder Revival ii: the twentieth Century and its Repertoire', in ed. Thomson, J.M., *The Cambridge Companion to the Recorder*, (Cambridge: Cambridge University Press 1995), p153
85  MacMillan, D., 'Arnold Dolmetsch and the Recorder Revival', *The Consort* LXIII (2007), pp90-104

*The Recorder In The Nineteenth Century*

Arnold Dolmetsch concluded his fine work *The Interpretation of Music of the XVIII and XVIII Centuries* with the words 'We can no longer allow anyone to stand between us and the composer': seminal thoughts to fire the minds of his doubting contemporaries.

## JOSEPH COX BRIDGE AND THE CHESTER RECORDERS

In 1886 the Chester Archaeological Society moved to new premises, and amongst the artefacts discovered in the removal was a case (which disintegrated rapidly) containing six recorders – four of which formed a set, now known as the Chester recorders - by Peter Bressan (1663-1731) one of the foremost recorder makers of his generation. The instruments were thought to have been in the possession of a Colonel Cholmondley who dwelt at the nearby Cholmondley Castle and were described by Bridge as soprano in f', alto in d', tenor in c' and bass in f.[86] Modern terminology would describe these instruments as alto, voice flute, tenor, and basset.

Beautiful as these instruments may be, for the purposes of the present work it is their early use in public performance which is of greatest interest. Joseph Cox Bridge (1853 – 1929) was organist of Chester Cathedral and took much interest in what are now referred to as the Chester recorders. In 1892 Bridge delivered a series of three lectures in the refectory of Chester Cathedral on the subject *Music of the Past* and in the first lecture made remarks about 'recorders or ancient flutes'. The recorders were used to play some Cheshire rounds, *The Blue Bells of Scotland*, and the *Cheshire Waif*. As has been related above, Arnold Dolmetsch assisted at the third of these lectures, but not upon the recorder. Some confusion exist in the literature regarding the 1892 use of the Chester recorders: Kirnbauer describes a performance on that occasion of a gavotte by Henri le Jeune,[87] and Thomson lists the players as Finn, Radcliffe, Bedford, and Bridge himself.[88] Both these authors quote from Hunt's *The Recorder and its Music* but the present author believes that they are confusing the 1892 and 1901 performances, the latter being discussed below.[89]

On February 12th. 1901 Bridge delivered a lecture on the Chester recorders to the Musical Association(footnote 83 above). He discussed the instruments and their history, his lecture being illustrated with the performance of the above-mentioned gavotte by Henri le Jeune (1526-1600), a duet for alto and basset recorders, and a quartet composed for the occasion by Bridge himself (see Chapter VI). This piece was almost certainly the first to be composed for recorders in the twentieth century: the players were the flautists A.J.Finn and J.Radcliffe, with the Revd. J.L. Bedford (a player of the Welsh pibcorn) and

---

86   Bridge, J.C., 'The Chester Recorders', *Proceedings of the Musical Association*, XXVII (1901), pp109-120
87   Kirnbauer, M., Das war Pionierarbeit-die Bogenhauser Künstlerkapelle, ein frühes Ensemble alte Musik, p43
88   Thomson, J.M., 'The Recorder Revival i: the friendship of Bernard Shaw and Arnold Dolmetsch' in *The Cambridge Companion to the Recorder*, p143
89   Hunt, E.H., *The Recorder and its Music*, p122-3

Bridge himself. Many years later Edgar Hunt had converse with Dr. Bridge, who told him that the players did not properly understand the fingering required, and treated the recorders like whistles, covering the thumb- holes with stamp- paper.

During the lecture Bridge commented that he believed that music for the recorder was 'of a very simple character, and confined, more or less, to an octave of notes'. This is surprising, for in subsequent sentences he observes (having studied Salter's *The Genteel Companion; or Exact Directions for the Recorder* of 1683) that higher notes may be obtained by 'pinching' the thumb-hole. A disparity here becomes apparent: Bridge's own lecture shows a perception of the function of the thumb-hole, yet his conversation with Hunt suggests that he was unaware of this. An examination of a copy of the Bridge quartet (kindly supplied to the present author by the Chester Archaeological Society) reveals that the first part (for alto recorder in f') utilizes the note g", which requires an open thumb-hole. The present writer has explored, on his recorder, the possibility of an alternative fingering for g" which does not involve an open thumb-hole and has found no satisfactory option for sounding this note. The three lower parts of Bridge's piece are all confined to one octave and would be played with the thumb-hole occluded. The likely conclusion is either that the young Hunt misunderstood the older musician, or that the latter's memory was inaccurate.

The discussion which ensued after Bridge's paper ranged through the pitch of the recorders, the etymology of the term 'recorder', the wood from which the instruments were made, and subsequently to Handel's use of the recorder contrasted with his use of the transverse flute. Christopher Welch noted that the obbligato to *O Ruddier than the Cherry* from Handel's *Acis and Galatea* was scored for 'flauto piccolo', Welch considering this instrument to have been a fipple (duct) flute.[90] The passage in question has a compass of two octaves but this, surprisingly, did not evoke comment in view of Bridge's earlier assertion that recorder music generally had a compass of about one octave.

The Chester recorders came to London again for the Music Loan Exhibition in 1904, and were eventually re-tuned and re-voiced by Carl Dolmetsch in 1939: their poor state of voicing and intonation combined with the players' lack of knowledge of recorder technique must have led the to performances of 1892 and 1901 verging on the cacophonous. However, a poorly-understood instrument was beginning to emerge from obscurity, and the organist from Chester deserves his place in the roll of those who brought about the renaissance of the recorder and its music.

---

[90] Welch, C., *Six Lectures on the Recorder and other Flutes in Relation to Literature*, pp123-127

*The Recorder In The Nineteenth Century*

## CARL ENGEL

The German organologist Carl Engel (1818 –1882) came to London in the mid-1840s and acquired an extensive collection of instruments, which, after his death, was bequeathed to the Victoria and Albert Museum and to the Royal College of Music. Engel's work prompted the South Kensington Exhibition of Ancient Musical Instruments in 1872 and his catalogue for this exhibition became a standard catalogue in what was to become the Victoria and Albert Museum, only being replaced in 1968. His catalogue gives a useful insight into the position of the recorder in the 1870s:

> but not many are likely to have seen a recorder, as it has now become very scarce.[91]

Engel possessed a curious tenor recorder now in the Victoria and Albert Museum, London, (285-1882) by Goulding (c1786-1834): the instrument is discussed in Chapter III (recorder N15). The peculiarities of this instrument engendered considerable controversy (and indeed confusion – see the notes on the instrument in Chapter III): much of the debate was resolved by Christopher Welch in his 1898 lecture to the Musical Association.

## CHRISTOPHER WELCH

The bibliophile Christopher Welch's role in the history of the recorder is perhaps more literary than musical, but his six lectures delivered to the Musical Association mark a further step in the growing interest in the instrument. Welch (1832-1915) delivered the first of his lectures in 1898, the series being published in 1911. The six lectures bore the titles:
1. Literary errors on the subject of the recorder
2. Tone and effect of the recorder
3. Hamlet and the recorder
4. Shakespeare's allusions to flutes and pipes
5. Milton on flutes and flute-players
6. The temple flute-player and the tomb-piper

Lecture I discussed the terminology of the instrument and the uncertainty (to a late nineteenth century author) surrounding its nature. Welch proceeded to describe the instrument from the time of Chaucer in the late Middle Ages, mentioning important writers on the instrument (Agricola, Praetorius, and Mersenne) as well as King Henry VIII and

---

91    Engel, C., *Musical Instruments in the South Kensington Museum*, (London: Eyre and Spottiswoode 2nd. ed. 1874), p122

referred to the puritan attack on the flute. He discussed several terms for the recorder, its treatises, and the decline of the instrument – 'decay and extinction'. He castigates the eighteenth century historians Burney and Hawkins before discussing the apparent errors of Carl Engel and William Chappell, the latter authors being criticized (and corrected) for their opinions on the Goulding tenor mentioned above.

Lecture II dealt with the tone and use of the recorder, Handel's use of the 'flute' and the obbligato to *O Ruddier than the Cherry* (a similar discussion followed Bridge's lecture in 1901, in which Welch took part). The two subsequent lectures were essentially confined to Shakespeare, the fifth to Milton, and the final lecture to matters of Jewish religious practice.

The published edition of Lecture III illustrates the four 'Chester' recorders and a renaissance-pattern tenor recorder (probably by Bassano) lent to Welch by Messrs. Rudall Carte: a copy of this (or a similar) instrument made by Rudall, Carte &.Co. is held in the Bate Collection at Oxford (D10). Welch notes the distinction between the two-jointed sixteenth and seventeenth century instrument and the multi-jointed baroque recorders of Bressan.

Welch's lectures brought a depth of perception to the organology of the recorder and he dismissed a number of misconceptions which existed at the time.

## JOHN FINN

The flautist A.J. Finn played a small part in the revival of the recorder for he played one of the 'Chester' recorders during Bridge's 1901 lecture, and in 1904 delivered a lecture entitled *The Recorder, Flute, Fife, and Piccolo* as part of a series given during the Music Loan Exhibition of 1904.[92] Finn discussed the characteristic features of the recorder and gave a brief outline of its history. He observed that the recorder band existed in former times in Belgium, but it is tempting to speculate that he may have been influenced by the performance on recorders by students from Brussels of a 'March of Les Lansquenets' at the International Inventions Exhibition in 1885 (see below). Finn refers to Welch's paper before mentioning Humphrey Salter's *The Genteel Companion* of 1683 (see above, J.C. Bridge) and illustrated this part of his lecture with a performance (on a tenor recorder) of *Haile to the Mertaille Shades* from *The Genteel Companion*. He ascribes the decline of the recorder to its limited compass, limited volume, and 'defective intonation'. At the end of his lecture Finn commented that:

> Undoubtedly there was something attractive about the old flutes. We are still interested in them, but they are of the past.

---

[92] *English Music 1604-1904, being the Lectures given at the Music Loan Exhibition of the Worshipful Company of Musicians, held at Fishmongers' Hall, London Bridge, June-July 1904*, (London: The Walter Scott Publishing Co.Ltd. 1906 also New York: C.Scribner's Sons 1906), pp120-163

The redevelopment of old instruments had yet to come about – at least in the eyes of this flautist, who, unlike most of his contemporaries – had a certain familiarity with the recorder.

## FRANCIS WILLIAM GALPIN

Cast in the unlikely mould of country clergyman and musical scholar, Canon Galpin was born (as was Arnold Dolmetsch) in 1858. A priest of the Church of England, he became Vicar of Hatfield Broad Oak in Essex in 1891 and remained in that benefice until 1915. Galpin died in 1945 and the Galpin Society for the study of old musical instruments was established in his memory and continues to be of importance in the field of organology. During his lifetime, Galpin amassed a collection of some 500-600 musical instruments of all types, building some himself; most of the collection was sold to the Museum of Fine Arts, Boston, in 1916 and the recorders remain in that collection. To the student of the recorder he is important both as a maker and player of the instrument in the early days of its revival: the subsequent criticisms of these performances again reflect the common perception of the instrument and other early instruments whose playing techniques were but imperfectly understood.

Galpin's first checklist (1881-1890) includes four recorders, including one by Stanesby and one by Prowse (fl1816-1868), although subsequent study reveals this latter instrument to be a four-keyed flageolet: it is currently in the Museum of Fine Arts, Boston (17.1840).[93]

Galpin was apparently sufficiently familiar with the recorder by 1890 to play it in public for he and his wife gave musical illustrations to accompany a lecture by C.F.Ashby Williams on *Music common in England during the days of Good Queen Bess*. A report in *The Musical World* of 22nd. November 1890 makes interesting reading:

Illustrations were also played by Mr. Galpin upon the Recorder, which may be described as a bass flute of soft and rich tone quality, but played *à bec* on a waite[94], practically a flageolet and from which we derive our title for certain persons who make night hideous at Christmastime and (also) the original of the cornet[95], a straight, conical, tube with lateral holes. The effect of *Ein feste Burg* played on the latter instrument and accompanied by the regal is indescribable and fully accounts for our ancestors' partiality for instruments of the stringed variety.

---

[93] Galpin, B., 'Canon Galpin's Checklists', *Galpin Society Journal* XXV (1972), pp4-21
[94] waite = wite, an old English word for punishment
[95] The instrument in question was probably a mute cornett, the straight form of the cornett or zink. It is hardly the precursor of the brass cornet, which was derived from the trumpet.

Galpin's extensive collection of historical instruments was enhanced by the inclusion of instruments of his own making or finishing: Randall reported that Galpin 'had exact and playable facsimiles made of the rarer instruments, rackets, shawms, and cromornes, to name a few'.[96] Of particular interest is a set of four renaissance-type recorders, now in the Museum of Fine Arts, Boston (17.1805-8 [N7-10]). Bessaraboff, in his introduction to his description of these instruments, writes:

> Canon Galpin kindly supplied the following information about the reproduction of the recorders Nos. 56, 57, 58, and 59.
>
> As a large number of old specimens passed through my hands when I was helping Mrs. Crosby Brown to form her collection, I was able to take measurements of bore, etc., of some of the less common wind instruments. I also was in correspondence with the authorities of continental museums (which I knew personally) and found them willing to send me details of others. Having drawn all out to scale, I got one or other of the English wind-instrument-making firms to make the body of the instrument with the correct bore. Then I fitted the instrument up with the necessary finger-holes and brass keys, as shown in the work of Praetorius and Mersenne. From this you can see that they are not *facsimiles* of any particular specimen, but playable reproductions of the old types. I required them for practical use and many of them have been played at lectures in London and elsewhere, even the Great Bass Shawm (No.132), which the late Sir Frederick Bridge of Westminster Abbey delighted in.
>
> Specifically, Canon Galpin stated that Nos. 56 and 57 were made in London and finished by him; No.58 is the 'reproduction of a sixteenth century instrument in my present collection'; and No.59 is a reproduction of the type found at Verona, Brussels, Berlin, Vienna. (A letter from Canon Galpin, January 21, 1936).[97]

These recorders were exhibited at the Fishmonger's Hall Exhibition of 1904 (see below) and illustrated in Galpin's *Old English Instruments of Music* of 1910.

Galpin was an enthusiastic promoter of musical events in his village community, forming both an amateur orchestra and a choir. In 1893 he organized a function for children *Ye Olde Englishe Pastymes* with simple music, but recorders were not employed. In 1897 he presented the first of his 'Paraffin Concerts' to raise money in aid of electric lighting in the town (then provided by private enterprise), and in 1901 gave a 'Concert of works historical to show the progress of ordinary music 1685-1828', but again there is no evidence for the use of recorders.

It is in the Paraffin Concert of 1904 that we first read of the Galpin Recorder Quartet. The instruments were those completed by Galpin, being a treble in g', an alto in d', tenor in g', and bass in c (in modern terminology alto, voice flute, basset, and bass). The music performed is not

---

[96] Randall, F.G., 'F.W.G. 1858-1945', *Galpin Society Journal* 1 (1948), pp5-9
[97] Bessaraboff, N., *Ancient Musical Instruments: an Organological Study of the Musical Instruments in the Leslie Lindsay Mason Collection at the Museum of Fine Arts, Boston*, pp68-69

known, but in 1905 a similar concert was given and included an Ayre *O Mistress Mine* and 'A Galiard [sic] c1600'. The parish chronicler observed that 'The recorders were pleasingly quiet and formed a complete contrast to the more assertive music of the present day'. Curiously, Godman also alludes to a comment by the chronicler in 1903 'This was a unique performance reminding us of the time when soft music was admired more than volume of sound' yet there is no mention of the use of recorders in that year.[98]

Galpin was a remarkable musician - a cleric cast in the role of an accomplished organologist and antiquarian, a man who was a pioneering enthusiast in the revival of what we now call early music. In relation to the recorder, he was one of the first to sound the instrument in public in England, and appears to have been the first man in England to produce playable recorders at the turn of the nineteenth and twentieth centuries. It is seldom appreciated that Galpin was playing recorder quartets in public almost a quarter of a century before Dolmetsch introduced recorder consorts at Haslemere.

## THE EXHIBITIONS

The late nineteenth and early twentieth centuries witnessed substantial international exhibitions in several European cities. Some of these featured both historic and contemporary musical instruments with some exhibitions being devoted entirely to matters musical. The appearance of recorders at these exhibitions (and the increasing numbers in which they were displayed) serves to highlight a growing interest in the rediscovery of early music and instruments: it should be recalled that, at least in England, the recorder was virtually unknown in the middle of the nineteenth century. The following paragraphs serve to describe the London exhibitions.

### 1872

An exhibition of ancient musical instruments was mounted in 1872 at the South Kensington – later Victoria and Albert – Museum under the direction of Carl Engel. In the preface to the catalogue Engel noted that an increasing number of collections of musical instruments was coming to light in Europe and made the observation that recorders were 'very scarce' (see above, Carl Engel). Nine recorders were displayed at the exhibition, most being of eighteenth century origin, the recorders being variously described as English flutes, flûtes à bec, flauti dolci, and recorder. Engel himself lent an 'English Flute or Flûte à bec about 1700' and an English recorder of the seventeenth century described as a 'species of flute'. It is likely that the former instrument is a tenor recorder by Goulding described above as

---
[98] Godman, S., 'Francis William Galpin – Music Maker' *Galpin Society Journal* XII (1959), pp8-16

'English flute or Flûte à bec about 1700' (N15 in the inventory) and Rudall Carte lent an 'Old English Flute or Flûte à bec' which may be the instrument illustrated in the report of Welch's 1902 lecture to the Musical Association. An elegant anonymous recorder covered with tortoiseshell with gold piqué and mother of pearl inlay which was reputedly the property of the composer Giachino Rossini (1792-1868) was also shown: it remains in the Victoria and Albert Museum (1124.1869). It is not known whether or not Rossini actually played the recorder.

The 1872 exhibition appears to have marked the re-appearance of the recorder in England: confusion regarding the terminology of the instrument (which continued for some years) is evident in the several appellations applied to the instrument which would be soon known simply as 'recorder'.

### 1885

The International Inventions Exhibition took place between May and November 1885 at the Royal Albert Hall, the musical events being collated by A.J.Hipkins. Hipkins (1826-1903) was a keyboard player, musicologist and instrument collector, a friend and supporter of Arnold Dolmetsch, and one of the first in England to give recitals on the harpsichord. For the exhibition, Hipkins assembled a large collection of instruments, autograph manuscripts, paintings, letters, and other artefacts relating to music and, in addition to the static exhibition, concerts of vocal and instrumental music were given. Both the display of instruments[99] and the recitals[100] are of interest in the history of the recorder.

Twenty-two recorders were displayed, including eighteenth century instruments by the Rottenburg family, Coppens, and Villars. Fourteen had been lent by the Belgian collector Cesar Snoeck (1825-1899) and, as in 1872, terminology was inconsistent.

On the first, second, and fourth of July concerts of 'Ancient Music' were given under the direction of Victor-Charles Mahillon of the Brussels Conservatoire. The instruments played included harpsichord, viola da gamba, regal, and one-keyed flute, the latter instrument being played by Dumon, who also directed a group of eight students playing recorders. This appears to have been the first 'modern' performance on recorders in

---

[99] Hipkins, A.J., *Catalogue of the Loan Exhibition of Musical Instruments, Manuscripts, Books, Paintings, and Engravings, exhibited in the Gallery and lower Rooms of the Albert Hall*, (London: William Clowes and Sons 1885)

[100] *Programmes of the International Inventions Exhibition May 4th – November 9th 1885* (London: William Clowes and Sons 1885)

*The Recorder In The Nineteenth Century*

England and provoked a mixed response on the part of the critics. The instruments played were copies of a set of renaissance recorders by Kynseker (c1636-1686) in the Germanisches Nationalmuseum in Nuremburg made by Mahillon and which remain in Le Musée Instrumental de Musique in Brussels (N31-38).

In the programme (price 1d.) for the concerts is written:

6. Sinfonia Pastorale 'Euridyce'          I.Peri
Eight flauti dolci by pupils of M.Dumon's class. The above *to which was sometimes added a drum* composed the military music of the Band of Lansquenets of the sixteenth century.

10. March of the Lansquenets
(of the time of the peace of Cambrai 1519)

Eight flauti dolci and a drum by the pupils of Mons. Dumon's class[101]

The reactions to these performances were somewhat equivocal. The *Musical Times* of August 1st. 1885 noted that the performers exercised a large amount of skill but:
> From the point of view of abstract musical effect, the efforts of the players varied greatly. Some of the effects were beautiful as well as curious, while others were only curious. In the latter category must be placed the sound produced by the eight flauti dolci in a Sinfonia Pastorale from *Eurydice* by Jacopo Peri, a composer generally considered he originator of opera. The flauti dolci are flutes à bec of various lengths, the lowest or bass flute extending downwards to F. [this is given in stave notation in the original] These instruments, with sometimes the addition of a drum, formed the band of the Lansquenets of the sixteenth century. The pupils of M.Dumon's class handled them well, but the effect resembled a description of street organ now happily but rarely heard.[102]

The vitriolic George Bernard Shaw (then a music critic and who subsequently became a friend to Arnold Dolmetsch) was even less enthusiastic. Writing in *The Dramatic Review* of 4th. July 1885 (reproduced in *Shaw's Music*[103]) he reported:
> The original members of the Band of Lansquenets, of the XVI century, are happily dead; but they have left their flutes and drum behind them. The drum is of the sort used by the *virtuosi* that accompany Punch and Judy shows; and the flutes

---

101   Programme of the Internatiol Invention Exhibition
102   *Musical Times* XXVI 1st. August 1885
103   Shaw, G.B., *Shaw's Music: the Complete Musical Criticism in 3* Volumes ed. Lawrence, D.H., (London: The Bodley Head 1981), p302

are brown keyless flageolets,[104] not very accurately pierced, and not absolutely identical in pitch. They are of various sizes, the largest resembling the leg of an old-fashioned bed, and the smallest – a most dreadful instrument – a leg of the small stool belonging to the same suite of furniture. They are eight in family, and when they discoursed the March of the Lansquenets at the Historic Concerts in the International Exhibition, the effect was voted 'quaint'. The incessant beating of the loosely stretched drumhead; the weak whistling of the soprano flutes; and the mournful woodiness of the tenors and basses moving in thirds, fifths, and sixths with them – all being more or less out of tune from defects of construction that no skill on the part of the performers could neutralize – made a whole which was certainly quaint enough: almost as quaint as the waits at Christmastide. But a little of it was enough to go a long way. These Lansquenet flutes are called *flauti dolci*, or sweet flutes...The 'sweet flute' has an inimitable plaintive silliness that is all its own; but it is not sweet.

Hipkins recalled the performances in his *Musical Instruments* of 1888:

In the same concerts M.Dumon and his pupils played a march of the Lansquenets (1519) on eight flûtes douces (*flauti dolci*), in parts, accompanied by a drum. This was the military music of the period.[105]

It is not without possibility that both Shaw and the anonymous *Musical Times* reviewer were correct in their disparaging remarks, yet viewed from the distance of history certain observations may be made. Firstly, the instruments themselves were copies by Mahillon of seventeenth century recorders and at this stage in his career Mahillon may not have been familiar with the intricacies of the bore, voicing, and tuning of the recorder, Shaw noting that the recorders being 'not very accurately pierced'. Secondly, no record appears to exist as to the source of the fingering used by the players and recorder fingerings in the past were neither standardized nor static. Thirdly, although many Victorians were fascinated by matters antiquarian, there was often a tendency to despise such things as being primitive. In passing, it should be noted that a question mark must hang over the assertion that the band of the Lansquenets played recorders: transverse instruments (flutes or fifes) would have been more appropriate for out-of-doors performance.

The importance of these concerts lies not so much in their reported technical inaccuracy, but in the brave steps of Mahillon, Dumon, and Gevaert (director of the Brussels Conservatoire) to introduce the sound of forgotten instruments to the public: the recorder was not only seen – as in 1872 – but also heard.

---

104 The instruments were not flageolets but this term would have been more familiar to the readers than 'recorder': both French and English flageolets were usually keyed at this period (D.M.)
105 Hipkins, A.J., *Musical Instruments, Historic, Rare, and Unique* (Edinburgh: A. & C.Black 1888), p90

*The Recorder In The Nineteenth Century*

## 1890

The Royal Military Exhibition was held at Chelsea Town Hall, London, in 1890 and consisted largely of wind instruments. The catalogue mentions figures of significance in the history of the recorder including Virdung, Praetorius, Mersenne, Salter (author of *The Genteel Companion*) and Stanesby.[106] Seventeen recorders were exhibited, including the Mahillon Kynseker copies which had been played at the International Inventions Exhibition, and a further recorder from Belgium which was described as a 'Great Bass Flûte Douce in C, an exact reproduction of an instrument in the Musée du Steen in Antwerp'. Although not so described in the catalogue, the instrument is probably a copy by Mahillon, recorder N41: the original remains in Antwerp, the collection now being housed in the Vleeshuis Museum. The Musical World of 8th. November 1890 reported on a lecture by J.A.Keppey given in connection with the exhibition on the history of military musical instruments. Keppey commented on the presence of the recorders, 'the flûte douce and the flûte à bec' and noted that several fine specimens were exhibited. There is no evidence to suggest that the recorders were played: the term 'flûte douce' was widely applied in the catalogue.

## 1904

The Worshipful Company of Musicians organized a large 'Music Loan Exhibition' at the Fishmongers' Hall in London in the summer of 1904, the lavish catalogue (limited to 500 copies) containing general information and illustrations as well as a description of the exhibited instruments.[107] On page 176 there is a paragraph devoted to the history of the recorder:

> The modern transverse flute was preceded by the flute with a fipple mouth-piece, known as the fipple flute or recorder, or by the French name of flûte à bec, now surviving only in the flageolet or penny whistle...the lack of artistic quality in their tone fully accounts for their disappearance.

The un-named author appears to be unaware that a number of the exhibited recorders were of modern manufacture.

Recorders (page 181)

1. A set of Four Recorders. German
Treble in g', alto in d' tenor in g bass in c
[1600] Rev. F.W.Galpin

---

106 Day, C.R., *A Descriptive Catalogue of the Musical Instruments recently exhibited at the Royal Military Exhibition, London* (London: Eyre and Spottiswoode Ltd 1891)
107 See footnote 92

Recorder was a name given to the whistle flute in the fifteenth century and continued in use till the early part of the eighteenth century when it became known as the Common or English Flute, to distinguish it from the transverse or German flute, and is now erroneously called the flageolet.

These recorders are illustrated, and appear identical to those in Galpin's *Old English Instruments of Music* and which are now in the Museum of Fine Arts, Boston. In the catalogue they are described as 'German' and their date is given in square brackets '[1600]'. The present author is of the opinion that this description (German [1600]) is given to illustrate a type of instrument in use in Germany at that period: it would be out of character for Galpin to give a false description of, or date for, his instruments.

2. Recorder in c', German, Seventeenth century.
Messrs. Rudall Carte.

This is probably the instrument illustrated in Welch's *Six Lectures* and of which there is a copy by Rudall Carte in the Bate Collection in Oxford (D10, Bate Collection 0116).

3. A set of four recorders, French, of eighteenth century origin

These are the 'Chester' recorders by Bressan and are of English manufacture: Bressan's biographical details have been the subject of debate in recent years and would probably not have been available in 1904.

During the course of the exhibition a series of seventeen lectures was given: that by A.J. Finn on 'The recorder, flute, fife, and piccolo' is quoted under the heading A.J.Finn (above). The lecture was illustrated with a short piece played on a tenor recorder but the particular instrument used is not specified.

In the 1870s the recorder was virtually unknown in England, an extinct instrument whose terminology (in several languages) was confusing: by the early twentieth century a few pioneers were studying the instrument and bringing it back to life. The revival of the recorder is intimately linked to the process of the revival of early music and this movement itself accelerated in pace as the nineteenth century drew to its conclusion. At first the recorder was used to illustrate lectures, but the performances at the International Inventions Exhibition formed part of a concert programme: however, it was not until the early years of the twentieth century that recorders were again featured in a concert. Public awareness of the instrument must have increased as a result of the exhibitions but – inevitably – the proclamation of research was restricted to academic musicological circles.

The critics were far from extolling the sound of the recorder, at best describing it as

## The Recorder In The Nineteenth Century

pleasing, and at the worst curious or even cacophonous. The poor reception of the re-born recorder requires comment, the fault not lying with the instrument itself or – often – its players. Firstly, recorder technique was evidently poorly understood despite the survival of several seventeenth and eighteenth century treatises. Secondly, the quality of the instruments (or their condition, for example, the 'Chester' recorders) may have left much to be desired. Shaw commented on the inaccurate 'piercing' of Mahillon's instruments but perhaps failed to realize that the skills of recorder voicing and tuning had been virtually unknown (certainly in England) for the best part of a century. It should also be noted that some of the early copies of recorders were essentially made as museum pieces, and intended more for exhibition than for public performance, and that many of the early makers did not possess the skill and intuition of Arnold Dolmetsch. Few of those who heard the sound of the recorder in the early days of its revival would have echoed Dolmetsch's words:

> At the first sound the recorder ingratiates itself to the hearer's affection. It is sweet, full, profound, yet clear, with just a touch of reediness.[108]

By the beginning of the twentieth century early instruments were becoming more common: Dolmetsch's concerts had made the viol and lute familiar to a small coterie of devotees, and music of the renaissance and early baroque was heard regularly at these performances. The recorder was never a particularly prominent instrument even in its heyday but in England the tide had begun to turn.

### FRANCE

The revival of the recorder in England is intimately bound to the activities of a handful of scholars: in France the study of the revival focuses more on places, collections, and an intriguing collection of recorders.

Two citations from the middle of the 1880s serve to introduce the manner in which the recorder was perceived at the time. Chouquet's catalogue of the instruments in the Conservatoire museum dating from 1886 lists instrument 386 (the first of some twenty-eight recorders) as follows:

> 386. Flûte à bec en ivoire
>
> La flûte à bec, qu'on appelait aussi *flûte douce* et *flûte d'Angleterre* a

---

[108] Dolmetsch, A., *The Interpretation of Music of the XVII and XVIII Centuries*, p457

longtemps été en faveur.[109] [The recorder, also known as the *'flûte douce'* and *'English flute'* was popular for a long time]
Jacquot's dictionary of 1886 gives two separate entries for la flûte douce:

Flûte douce. Ancienne flûte à bec du Moyen-Age. Appelle par les Italiens Flauto Dolce [An ancient flute from the middle ages. Called by the Italians the soft flute].
Flûte douce ou d'Angleterre. Cette flûte traversière avait neuf trous et fut employer dans les orchestras en Europe, jusqu'au siècle dernier. [110] [This transverse flute had nine holes and was used in European orchestras until the last century]

Jacquot does not appreciate that the recorder (whichever name it is given) is a vertical flute. The perception of the recorder as an instrument with only historical significance was evidently held on both sides of the English Channel.

## PARIS

An interest in collecting old musical instruments began in Paris in the late eighteenth century and in 1796 a room in the recently-opened Institut National de Musique (later the Conservatoire) was dedicated to a collection of old instruments, foreign instruments, and to good examples of contemporary instruments. Several enthusiasts began instrument collections (including small numbers of recorders) around the middle of the nineteenth century but some collectors (such as the composer Louis Clapisson) appeared more interested in exotica than in the revival of early music. The first of these specialized collections began in the 1840s but after the sale of Clapisson's collection to the state in 1861 old instruments became more accessible to the general public. Gétreau describes the last quarter of the nineteenth century as *'la haute époque'* [the high point] of instrument collecting in France, and concludes her paper with an appendix listing twenty-two collections from the nineteenth century, each holding more than forty instruments.[111] Such activity was not paralleled to the same extent in other countries and, although the recorders were few in number, they were at least being collected, catalogued, and displayed.

---

109 Chouquet, G., *Le Musée du Conservatoire Nationale de Musique. Catalogue descriptif et raisonnée*, (Paris: Libraire de Firmin, Diderot et Cie. 1884), p102
110 Jacquot, A., *Dictionnaire des Instruments de Musique*, (Paris: Libraire Fischbacher 2nd. edition 1886)
111 Gétreau, F., 'Alte Instrumente im Frankreich des 19 Jahrhunderts. Die Rolle des Conservatoire und privat Initiativen' in *Basler Jahrbuch für historische Musikpraxis*, (Wintherthur : Amadeus 1997), pp181-293

*The Recorder In The Nineteenth Century*

## L'EXPOSITION UNIVERSELLE 1889

It has already been noted that the late nineteenth century was an age of great international exhibitions. The 'Exposition Universelle' (May to November 1889) took place on a site near the Eiffel Tower, and was visited by several million people. Held in the centenary year of the Revolution, the exhibition showed France to be a nation of social and industrial progress: there were both historical and contemporary displays, and, of particular interest, an exhibition of old instruments and a series of five concerts featuring early music on period instruments. Two of these were devoted to French music, and two to Italian, with the fifth being given as an organ recital. Although recorders were not played, the use of other early instruments aroused much interest. Fausner has written extensively on the subject, and relates that, in the concerts of French music, the first part was devoted to modern works, the second to baroque.[112] The players were Louis Diémer (harpsichord), Jules Delsart (viola da gamba), the Belgian violinist Louis van Waefelghem (viola d'amore), and the flautist Claude Taffanel. With the exception of van Waefelghem, all were prominent teachers at the Paris Conservatoire. Taffanel – accompanied by harpsichord and viola da gamba - played pieces by Rameau at both concerts. The musicologist Julien Tiersot visited both the exhibition and its concerts, describing his experiences in his *Musiques Pittoresques. Promenades musicales à l'Exposition de 1889* and noted that Taffanel made the sound of his flute soft to give the impression of the recorders of former times.[113]

Tiersot observed the method of reaming an oboe (in a display by courtesy of the museum at La Couture-Boussey)[114] and also the history of the 'ancient family of recorders' (again courtesy of La Couture). Following a visit to the exhibition on June 8th, he expressed the hope that the old instruments would be revived from their mute condition, and that some artist, inspired by the spirit of the old makers of the viola d'amore and viola da gamba, would allow us to hear again the music of Bach, Rameau, Couperin, and Mozart on the old instruments.

Constant Pierre also gave an indication of the presence of recorders at the exhibition in his *La facture instrumentale à l'Exposition Universelle de 1889:* under the heading *L'Exposition Retrospective* he reported a variety of instruments, tools, and accessories, noting that many instruments had come from La Couture-Boussey.[115] There were many copies of recorders of the seventeenth century, flutes, and a flûte d'accord, but these were insufficient to portray adequately the history of the instrument. The only recorders

---

[112] Fausner, A., *De Arquelogica Músical. La Música barroco y La Exposition Universel de 1889*, in ed. Carreras, J.J., Martin, M.A., *Concierto barroco. Estudios sobre Música, Dramatugia, e Historia Cultura,*. (Logroño :Universidad de Rioja 2004)

[113] Tiersot, J., *Musiques pittoresques. Promenades musicales à l'Exposition Universelle de 1889*, (Paris : Libraire Fischbacher 1889), p10

[114] The activities of the museum at La Couture-Boussey are described below

[115] Pierre, C., *La facture instrumentale à l'Exposition universelle de 1989. Notes d'un musicien sur les instruments à soufflé humaine nouveaux et perfectionnées*, (Paris : Libraire de l'Art Independent 1890), pp281-2, 283

precisely identified were to be found in case no.39, wherein there were two recorders, around sixty-five centimetres in length, one a tenor with one key by Hotteterre (the family member is not specified) and one by Bizet (French maker, 1716- c1758).

The instruments from La Couture-Boussey may have been modern copies (see below) but at least two historical recorders were on display. Taffanel, at least, appears to have had some perception of the sound of the recorder.

## L'EXPOSITION UNIVERSELLE ET INTERNATIONALE 1900

A further *Exposition* was held eleven years later in Paris in 1900, a report by the committee organizing the musical exhibition being published the same year.[116]

As in 1889, an emphasis was placed on historical matters and six recorders were exhibited, including four from the Versailles collection of la Comtesse de Bricqueville. The soprano, alto, and tenor instruments were of unknown make, but the bass was by Hotteterre: the recorders were illustrated on page 11 of the report. All are of baroque pattern but there is little outward similarity between them. An ivory tenor recorder and a carved boxwood recorder were also displayed. On this occasion there appears to have been no involvement of the museum at La Couture-Boussey.

## LA SOCIETE DES INSTRUMENTS ANCIENS

The harpsichordist Louis Diémer founded La Société des Instruments Anciens in the 1890s and toured extensively in Europe. A further early music ensemble, La Société des Instruments Anciens Casadesus, was founded by the viola d'amore player Henri Casadesus in 1901.

These ensembles appear to be the earliest regular 'early music groups' in Paris, a city in which there was already a considerable interest in the choral music of the renaissance and baroque epochs. However, there is no evidence to support the use of recorders (or other woodwind instruments) by these ensembles.

## LA COUTURE-BOUSSEY

The Normandy village of La Couture-Boussey has been of considerable significance in the manufacture of woodwind instruments since the late seventeenth century, and there is evidence to suggest that instruments have been made in La Couture (and the

---

116  *Musée retrospectif de la classe 17/ instruments de musique, procédés et produits à L'Exposition Internationale de Paris 1900*, (Paris : André Eymeoud 1900)

neighbouring village of Ivry-la-Bataille) since the battle of Ivry in 1590. It is believed that the name 'Boussey' is derived from buis, the French word for boxwood, formerly a common timber in the locality and of importance in the manufacture of (particularly early) woodwind instruments. The home village of the Hotteterres remained – until the mid twentieth century – a centre of woodwind instrument manufacture and in 1887 the instrument makers of La Couture determined to found a museum to 'conserve all woodwind instruments, their parts, materials, and the tools used in their manufacture': it was to facilitate both theoretical and practical study. The museum would collect instruments – original or copies – in use before the sixteenth century and also instruments made from the sixteenth to the nineteenth centuries in order to establish an historical base, especially dealing with the history of instrument making in La Couture. It was intended also to show the progress achieved in the resolution of the difficulties encountered in developing modern instruments.[117] Many instruments were acquired from the local factories of Lot, Noblet, Thibouville and Martin: others were borrowed (to be either copied or restored) from the collections of Ernest Thoinan and the Belgian attorney Cesar Snoeck, including some fifteen instruments by the Hotteterres. Two of these were tenor recorders: replicas were made and the original instruments duly returned. A copy of an Hotteterre tenor remains in the museum, but it is imperative to realize that these instruments are not copies in the twenty-first century sense, for only the external form of the instrument was copied and not the bore. Abondance writes:

> Notons toutfois qu'il s'agit là de répliques pour la vue, puisque les perces des instruments originaux n'ont pas été fidelement respectées.

There was no concern to reproduce the instruments as playable reproductions (*les perces...n'ont pas été fidelement respectées* [the bore was not faithfully reproduced]): the instruments were only to be looked upon [*pour la vue*]. The philosophy of the collection was pedagogic rather than practical: it was to show the appearance of the instruments rather than to reproduce their sound.

The museum opened in 1888 and now contains some 300 instruments of which nine are recorders of nineteenth century origin. Eight of these are *reconstitutions* (reconstructions), two (at least) being copies of older recorders.

## THE FRENCH RECORDERS

Recorders continued to be made in France (albeit in very small numbers) throughout the nineteenth century but a cluster of instruments built at the end of the century are of particular interest and it is with these that the following paragraphs are concerned: unfortunately it is not possible to ascribe exact dates to many of the instruments for their

---

117  Abondance (Gétreau), F., Musiciens et musique en Normandie, *Bulletin de Centre Normande d'Histoire Musicale* no 6 (1ère trimestre 1981), pp5-7

makers are not known. The *reconstitutions* made for the museum at La Couture-Boussey between 1888 and 1896 are described above, but there remains a group of some twenty instruments (including several whose makers are identified) which are thought to be of late nineteenth century origin. The instruments are scattered in various collections, but many are held in Le Musée de la Musique in Paris, many of these being 'anonymous': they are listed in the Inventory (Chapter III), and are most probably linked with the early days of the recorder revival.

The catalogue of the firm Jérome Thibouville-Lamy of 1878 lists a series of *flûtes à bec*, priced by the dozen, with prices ranging from 18 to 24 francs. Large flutes with a similar description are also offered, as are *Articles Jouets d'Enfants, Flûtes à bec en métal.* All these instruments are remarkably cheap, a 5-keyed flute, for example, being priced at 27Fr. and a Boehm flute at 200Fr.[118] The low price of these *flûtes douces à bec* suggests that, as well as childrens' toys, they may have been intended for school or amateur use but there is no other evidence to support this speculation.

At present there is no indication of the use to which these nineteenth century recorders were put, but their very existence implies an early revival of the recorder in France: the similarity in shape of the five anonymous recorders to those of Colas and F Noblet is unlikely to be a coincidence. Overall, there is a high proportion of altos and tenors in the collections and, somewhat unexpectedly, a particularly high proportion of tenors.

In summary, there were two distinct schools of recorder-making in late nineteenth century France – the first purely for display in glass cases, the second for a more musical function.

Many amateur music societies are known to have flourished in the late nineteenth and early twentieth centuries, but there is no evidence for the use of the recorder in this particular musical *milieu*: however, as Edgar Hunt has observed, 'there are many amateurs who would be able to play the recorder but would never get a note out of a flute'. Could this be the reason why recorders were made in the closing years of the nineteenth century in France?

Apart from a handful of instruments made early in the nineteenth century, the recorder appears to have been little known in France in the 1880s yet France appears to have led the world in the production of recorders and their preservation in museums, whereas in England activity in the field of the recorder revival was concentrated in the hands of a few researchers who made very few recorders.

---

118  *Catalogue of the firm of Jérome Thibouville-Lamy*, (Paris: 1878)

## GERMANY

There is a sense in which the recorder did not have to be revived in Germany. As has been related in Chapter V, the tradition of recorder making continued in the Bavarian town of Berchtesgaden throughout the nineteenth century. However, the recorder was essentially forgotten in mainstream musical practice, von Gunterhausen observing in 1855 that the instrument was seldom heard: Moeck, writing in 1978, noted that the recorder was not used in serious music although he commented on the Berchtesgaden tradition but does not write of its continuous existence into the twentieth century and even twenty-first centuries.[119]

As in other European countries, instrument collections began to be assembled during the latter part of the nineteenth century. The Dutch 'cellist Paul de Wit (1852-1925) set up a collection in Leipzig in 1886, and subsequently attempted to sell the collection to the Leipzig authorities. He finally sold it in 1905 to a wealthy paper manufacturer in Cologne by the name of Wilhelm Heyer (1849-1913) who established the Heyer Museum of Musical History and also acquired the collection of Alessandro Klaus of Florence: both the de Wit and Kraus collections contained recorders. The Heyer collection eventually became the foundation of the Musical Instrument Museum of the University of Leipzig. The Germanisches Nationalmuseum at Nuremberg was founded in 1852, and in 1905 Christian Doebereiner (a gambist who played his instrument with a 'cello bow) founded Die Deutsche Vereinigung für alte Musik: in subsequent years Doebereiner was one of the first to employ recorders in Bach's second and fourth Brandenburg concerti and also in the *Actus Tragicus* (Cantata 106).

## THE BOGENHAUSER KÜNSTLERKAPELLE

The Bogenhauser Künstlerkapelle (the Bogenhauser artists' band) was almost certainly the first recorder ensemble to be formed in the early days of the instrument's rebirth. Kirnbauer presents an extensive account (summarized below) of the ensemble's activities in his paper *Das war Pionierarbeit*.[120]

Bogenhauser is a district of Munich, and the members of the ensemble were amateur musicians, most coming from an artistic background. The Nuremberg painter Konrad Weigund (1842-1897) came into possession of a number of early eighteenth century woodwind instruments (possibly from a deceased person's estate) and began to play them before moving to Munich. Together with Wilhelm Düll (1835-1887), Düll's wife and his son Heinrich, he formed what a contemporary described as *ein lustiges Quartett* (a cheerful

---

119    Moeck, H., 'Zur "Nachgeschichte" und Renaissance der Blockflöte', *Tibia* I (2) (1978) p16
120    Kirnbauer, M., 'Das war Pionierarbeit' (see footnote 19)

quartet) playing recorders (including a bass, played by Weigund) with a guitar: this group existed in the 1880s and one Georg Pezold (1865-1943, subsequently a member of the ensemble) wrote to his parents in 1887 to say that he had heard the sound of recorders in Heinrich Düll's garden in Bogenhauser. At *Fastnachts* (Shrove Tuesday) – probably in the next year, 1888 - it is known that Weigund, Düll, and Pezold appeared in costume playing recorders, but the Künstlerkapelle as such appears to date from around the year 1890. Over the years the membership of the ensemble underwent some changes (which are not relevant to the history of the recorder) but the instrumental 'line-up' changed little. The basic ensemble consisted of the unlikely combination of three recorders (mainly altos), a bass recorder, a guitar, a tromba marina, and drums.

In 1899 the Bogenhauser Künstlerkapelle took part in a chamber music evening in the Bayerisches Hof Hotel in Munich in which several string trio movements were performed together with a song cycle, a two-piano piece by Saint-Saens, and a piano trio by Haydn. The Bogenhausers' programme gives a picture of the sort of repertoire favoured by the ensemble at the time:

Presidential March von König Friedrich Wilhelm III

| | | |
|---|---|---|
| Minuet anon. | | (4 recorders, guitar, tromba marina & drums) |
| Ave Maria | Arcadelt | |
| | (4 recorders) | |
| Rondo | Mozart | |
| | (3 recorders) | |
| Polonaise | Pleyel | |
| York'scher Reiter-Marsch | | (4 recorders, guitar, tromba marina, and drums) |

In addition to the 'serious' repertoire, the Bogenhausers also played Alpine folk music and *lustige Feldmusik* [military music], acquiring an extensive library of parts arranged for their particular instrumental combination.

The Bayerisches Hof concert of 1899 was under the direction of the notable Munich musician Heinrich Scherrer (1865-1937), an early champion of the Bogenhauser Künstlerkapelle and later one of its members. In 1902 he wrote of the group *"Das war Pionierarbeit"* [that was pioneering work]. The Bogenhausers continued to perform in Munich until their disbandment at the beginning of the Second World War: they had become an established (if perceived as quaint) part of the Munich musical scene, playing at many concerts and functions.

The Bogenhausers played on recorders dating from the early eighteenth century by such makers as the Denners, Oberlender, and Bressan, and these (together with other instruments owned by the group), are listed by Kirnbauer. Many of the instruments were detailed by Young in his 1982 paper 'Some further instruments by the Denners'.[121]

One instrument belonging to the Bogenhausers is of especial significance in the story of the revival of the recorder. The Munich instrument maker Gottlieb Gerlach (1856-1909) attempted to copy an alto recorder by J.Denner in the ensemble's collection, this instrument almost certainly being the first 'modern' recorder to be made in Germany (N10). It is not of good quality, for, according to Kirnbauer, the knowledge of how to voice and tune a recorder had been lost for some 100 years.

There is little doubt that the Bogenhauser Künstlerkapelle was the first regular recorder ensemble in the early music revival. It could be argued (from a twenty-first century standpoint) that much of the Bogenhausers' practice was hardly an accurate realization of old music, but, in the days of this pioneering ensemble, the concepts of authenticity and historically-informed performance were only just beginning to emerge. Certainly in their early days the Bogenhausers stood in the very vanguard of their field, and seldom can an amateur group have been of such significance in the revival of both an historic instrument and of early music. As Scherrer said in 1902,' *Das war Pionierarbeit'.*

## BELGIUM

The saga of the early music movement and revival of the recorder followed different strands in the three countries hitherto examined: Brussels, an old town in the young state of Belgium, followed yet another path, distinguished by its conservatoire, by its museum, and by a number of perceptive musicians and musicologists.

## THE CONSERVATOIRE

The Conservatoire Royale de Musique grew out of the Royal School of Music, established in 1821. In 1833 François-Joseph Fétis was appointed Director, in the latter years of the century being succeeded by François-Auguste Gevaert: both men were interested in the revival of early music, Gevaert being the first to introduce the young Arnold Dolmetsch to ornamentation and early instruments. It was during Gevaert's time of office that Dolmetsch first heard recorders and that students from the Conservatoire visited London to play recorders at the International Inventions Exhibition of 1885. The culture of

---

121 Young, P., 'Some further Instruments by the Denners', *Galpin Society Journal* XXXV, (1982), pp77-85

early music was further enhanced by the appointment of Victor-Charles Mahillon to the post of curator of the newly-created Musée Instrumentale du Conservatoire Royale de Musique, now Le Musée des Instruments de Musique. The combination of directors and the enlarging collection of instruments provided a cultural environment in which early music and its instruments could be explored.

## FRANCOIS-JOSEPH FETIS

Although not playing a known part in the recorder revival, François-Joseph Fétis (1784-1871), composer, historian, and writer, was a major figure in the early days of the early music movement. Fétis' philosophy 'art does not progress, it merely changes' underpinned much of the early music revival in France and Belgium and allowed music to be judged by standards other than those of his own day. He was of the opinion that immersion in the musical past was in part a reaction to the great romantic composers of his own generation.

In his five-volume treatise *Histoire Générale de Musique,* Fétis gave a brief description of a number of duct flutes.[122] He described the galoubet and French flageolet before giving a more detailed exposition of the *flûte à huit trous* (recorder) and making mention of the sixteenth century authors Agricola, Virdung, and Ganassi. Fétis then proceeded to indicate the compass of the *discantus, tenor,* and *bassus* and observed that the complete consort consisted of four recorders. He commented on the *flûtes à neuf trous*, those recorders built with two alternative holes for the little finger of the lower hand, one of which would be filled with wax according to whether the player played right or left hand uppermost. Fétis acquired an extensive collection of instruments which formed the basis of the collection in Brussels: he was one of the earliest nineteenth-century authors to describe the recorder

## VICTOR-CHARLES MAHILLON

Mahillon was born in Belgium in 1841 and became curator of the new Conservatoire museum in 1879. He amassed a large collection of instruments including several recorders, and published an extensive catalogue, the style of which is copied to this day and was one of the first – if not the first – to make copies of historic recorders (and other instruments) in the late nineteenth century. Mahillon copied many recorders (N29-42) including the Nuremberg Kynseker instruments which were played in London in 1885: most of his instruments are of the renaissance pattern (like Galpin's), although why he

---

122   Fétis, F-J., *Histoire Générale de Musique*, (Paris : Libraire Firmin, Diderot et Cie. vol 5 1876), pp174-184

chose this pattern instead of the baroque type is not known. Mahillon died in 1924.

## CESAR SNOECK

The Belgian attorney and amateur musician Cesar Snoeck (c1825-1899) made a large collection of instruments, many of which were eventually distributed to museums in Brussels, St. Petersburg and Berlin. An illustration of Snoeck surrounded by various instruments was published in *Die Woche* in June 1902, recorders being clearly visible amongst the various stringed and wind instruments.

In Belgium the significant features in the revival of the recorder lie in the Conservatoire, its museum, and in the activities of men like Fétis, Gevaert, and Mahillon, all enthusiasts for old music. The credit for making the first recorders of the revival lies with Mahillon, who not only pre-dated the English and German makers but also caused the sound of the instrument to be heard in public.

## THE NETHERLANDS

In stark contrast to the current importance of Holland in the world of the recorder, the country was of little significance in the instrument's early revival.

Early music societies flourished in Rotterdam, Haarlem, and Utrecht from the 1840s but these focussed essentially on the large-scale choral works of Bach, Handel, and the Dutch composer Sweelinck (1562-1621). Performances were also given of renaissance choral music, but little interest appears to have been taken in the revival of early instrumental music.

As in England and France, exhibitions were mounted, the first to contain historic instruments being that at Delft in 1863: early collectors included J.C.Boers (Nijmegen and Delft) and D.F. Scheurleer (Amsterdam), both of these collections now being housed in The Hague.

Bouterse relates that a soprano recorder by Steenbergen (1676-1752, Amsterdam) was recovered from a shipwreck in the Netherlands in 1888. Nothing is known of the history of the instrument, but its foot joint had been lost and replaced by a crude piece of wood.[123] Whether or not attempts were made to play this instrument in the nineteenth century remains a matter of speculation.

## ITALY, SPAIN AND THE NORDIC COUNTRIES

---

123   Bouterse, J., personal communication 2003

In the southern European countries, there is no evidence for the use of the recorder in the early days of its revival.

Kenyon de Pascual has indicated that two recorders were offered for sale in Madrid in 1788, but she advises that there is no evidence for the use of recorders in Spain before the 1930s.[124]

In Italy the flageolet was sometimes called for, particularly in dance music and one flauto d'amore was converted into a 'recorder' by Bertani in the late eighteenth or very early nineteenth century (recorder D2).

The recorder appears to have been revived in Sweden and Denmark around the 1930s: there is no evidence for its use in these countries in the earlier years of the twentieth century.

## SUMMARY – THE RECORDER PLAYED AND DISPLAYED

References given in the text demonstrate that the recorder was poorly understood in the final quarter of the nineteenth century. Confusion raged over its terminology, and dictionaries of music proclaimed it as an entirely obsolete instrument. A growing interest in antiquarianism – and with it a growing interest in early music – led to the rediscovery of old instruments (often called 'ancient' instruments) and eventually not only were the old instruments collected, restored, and played, but also were copied.

France, England, Germany, and Belgium became the leading nations in the recorder revival. Although the pattern and focus of that revival took slightly different courses in the different countries, an interest in collecting, restoring, making, and playing historic instruments was common to all. The French displayed much ingenuity in collecting and exhibiting recorders as well as making 'display copies' for museums. As has been noted above, a few playable instruments were made in France late in the nineteenth century. In England, scholars attempted to study the role of the recorder in former times and illustrate their lectures with live performances on the instruments, an antiquarian approach tempered with an enthusiasm to hear the old instruments as well as to exhibit them. Overall, the academic focus differed on the two sides of the English Channel with the French possessing more of a museum culture whilst the English took a more studious approach to the instrument and in reviving instrumental music of the renaissance. In Belgium the Conservatoire was the focus for collecting, making, and playing old instruments, Mahillon's work being of particular importance in the fields of both instrument-making and classification. Germany – which led the world in the Bach revival – was of less significance in the renaissance of the recorder despite the notable exception of the isolated activities of the Bogenhauser Künstlerkapelle.

It is not possible to consider the recorder revival in isolation from the whole growing early music culture, the recorder being only one instrument of many to excite the interest of the early pioneers. The early music revival in itself cannot be considered in isolation from

---

[124] Kenyon de Pascual, B., personal communications 2003, 2004

other historicist movements in the visual arts, architecture, and literature. As in so many 'revivalist' movements, activity appears to have developed spontaneously and synchronously in several countries. It would be reasonable to assert that if it were not for the revival of other early instruments by Dolmetsch, Galpin, the Bogenhausers and their contemporaries, the recorder may have lain buried by the dust of antiquity for many more years. The new age of the recorder was beginning to dawn when Dolmetsch bought his first recorder on June 7th. 1905 yet few, if any, could have foretold the subsequent story of the little eight-holed flute whose ancestry could be traced back to the Middle Ages.

## POSTSCRIPT

The phrase 'revival of the recorder' well describes the work of the early pioneers and suggests a restoration of the instrument to its traditional role in music of former times, whether that be the renaissance consort or the exuberant solo music of the baroque. The history of the recorder revival described in the preceding chapters would suggest that this was the intention of Dolmetsch and his contemporaries, but music, like time, does not stand still. Throughout the twentieth century the recorder acquired new roles both as a phenomenally successful educational tool, an instrument upon which many amateurs could attain a modicum of skill, and as a vehicle for avant-garde composers.

A hundred years after its tentative rebirth, the recorder has not only regained its historic role in the performance of early music, but has progressed to fresh fields and pastures anew.

# CHAPTER X

# OBSOLETE AND ECLIPSED?

The tale of the recorder in its dark age has been related, and it now remains to summarize the situation as it appears in the year 2007. It has been observed that the recorder declined in use after the middle of the eighteenth century and that this decline may be attributed to the changes in musical culture as the *style galant* of the baroque gave way to Sonata Form, as the small court bands of the baroque gave way to the increasingly large symphony orchestras of the late classical period. The recorder was hardly modified during this period of its history and its (already uncommon) place in the orchestra was totally superseded by the transverse flute, an instrument with considerable potential for development. Music had moved on but the gentle recorder remained static. The instrument had all but disappeared by the end of the eighteenth century yet Carl Dolmetsch's belief 'that it lingered on here and there' is confirmed by the present organological study of the recorder in the nineteenth century.

The inventory of recorders forms the kernel of the hypothesis that the recorder continued in use throughout the nineteenth century, for, without the instruments as proof, there would be no cause to postulate. Sixty-eight recorders are identified by maker, whilst a further forty-seven are classified as of unknown maker: nine instruments made at the turn of the eighteenth and nineteenth centuries are also included, as are twenty-three instruments of uncertain parentage, location or of organological curiosity. It is unlikely that the inventory is complete for inevitably there will be other recorders in small museums or private collections, but nevertheless it provides ample evidence for the continued existence of the recorder in northern Europe during the nineteenth century. Of particular interest is the preponderance of fifth and sixth flutes made in Bavaria and northern Austria, whereas altos and tenors predominated in other centres of recorder-making such as London, Paris, and La Couture-Boussey. Towards the latter years of the century, makers began to make copies of old recorders, some of these being purely for display purposes, yet others were made as functioning musical instruments: these activities occurred across northern Europe. The small recorders from Berchtesgaden are of particular interest, for work by the present author has shown that recorders have been made in the town in unbroken tradition from the late sixteenth century to the present day – a unique phenomenon in the history of the instrument.

Little music composed specifically for the recorder during the nineteenth century has been identified. This, in itself, is hardly surprising for few recorders were being made and documented instances of their use are few and far between, but from a stance outside the period it is possible to speculate that those recorders which remained in playing condition would have been used to play surviving eighteenth-century repertoire, music written for other instruments, or folk music.

An interest in the performance of music of former times accelerated in pace across Europe throughout the course of the nineteenth century: choral and instrumental works by composers of the renaissance and baroque were sought out, edited, and performed and late in the nineteenth century players began to explore historical instruments. The pioneers of the early music revival were not unduly concerned with matters of authenticity and historically-informed performance, such praxis eventually growing out of musicological study during the twentieth century. The revival of the recorder has now been shown to be a pan-European phenomenon and emerging – together with other 'early' instruments - from the culture of the early music revival. The recorder revival had begun to gather momentum by the time Arnold Dolmetsch purchased his Bressan alto recorder in 1905, yet there appears to have been little widespread use of the instrument until after the First World War, when a growing interest in the instrument became apparent, particularly in England and Germany. By the 1930s the recorder was established across Europe and America as an instrument for school children, amateurs, and a growing corpus of professional players, a movement founded upon research by the nineteenth century pioneers and fuelled by the growing availability of both high quality and of inexpensive instruments.

## EPILOGUE

It has now been demonstrated beyond reasonable doubt that the recorder, far from becoming extinct, maintained a shadowy existence throughout the nineteenth century: partially eclipsed by its cousin the transverse flute, obsolescent yet not obsolete - but not, as is so often supposed, buried in the mire of antiquity. The continued manufacture of recorders - albeit in minute numbers – testifies to an interest in, and awareness of, the instrument even though documented instances of its use are few and far between. In the form of the Berchtesgadner Fleitl the recorder enjoyed an Indian summer in Bavaria, this remarkable little instrument building a bridge between the guilds of wood-turners of the renaissance and baroque and the craftsmen of today. By the closing years of the nineteenth century the die had been cast for the recorder's resurrection from the edge of obsolescence to its new flowering in the twentieth century. Almost certain death had been transfigured into new birth. The simplicity of the recorder would appeal – as never before – to children, their teachers, and to amateurs of all ages, whilst its infuriating complexity would again fascinate the minds and fingers of erudite musicians. The wheel – as so often in the aeons of history – would turn full circle.

# ADDENDUM

Shortly before this book went to the printer, I received an e-mail from the Norwegian recorder player Svein Egil Skotte, drawing my attention to the existence of seventeen recorders in Norway which appeared to be of nineteenth-century origin. A tradition of playing folk music on recorders existed in Norway, particularly in the valley of Numedal. The instruments were called 'sea flutes' because they had come by sea from mainland Europe: four of the recorders (which are mainly alto-sized and are of plain outline) bear the stamp 'Schlosser', suggesting that they were made in Vogtland (Germany) by a member of the Schlosser family who were active from the first third of the nineteenth century (Thalheimer[125]). The dates of the first active member of the dynasty (Johann Gabriel Schlosser sen.) are not known, but his younger son Gustav Adolph (b1845) is described as *Pfeiffenmacher* (pipe-maker). The family continued to produce recorders until the 1970s.

It may be that a parallel can be drawn between the recorders in this small Norwegian valley and those of Berchtesgaden: in both places the instrument continued in use through the nineteenth century, principally, it appears, as an instrument upon which to play folk music.

I have just been notified by Mats Krouthen, Curator of Musical Instruments in the Ringve Museum (Norway) of the existence of three recorders from the nineteenth or very early twentieth century - a 478mm instrument by Adler of Markneukirchen c1900, a one-keyed soprano (310mm) of ?English origin 1800s, and a six-keyed 305mm blackwood recorder with straight foot-joint ?1800s.

---

125 [125] Thalheimer, P., 'Blockflötenbau in der Anonymität: Die familie Schlosser aus Zwota', *Tibia* 2005 (2) pp427-432

*The Recorder In The Nineteenth Century*

# BIBLIOGRAPHY

## THE RECORDER IN THE NINETEENTH CENTURY

Barnes, R., 'The Recorder 1740-1900 – obsolete and eclipsed?, unpublished M Mus diss., University of London 2001

MacMillan, D., 'The recorder in the late eighteenth and early nineteenth centuries', unpublished FTCL diss., 1982

MacMillan, D., 'The Recorder in the late eighteenth and early nineteenth Centuries', *The Consort* XXXIX 1983 pp489-497 (summary of FTCL diss.)

MacMillan, D., 'The Recorder 1800 – 1905', unpublished PhD diss., University of Surrey 2005

Moeck, H., 'Zur Nachgeschichte und Renaissance der Blockflöte', *Tibia* III (1) 1978 pp79-88

## ORGANOLOGY

Betz, M., *Der Csakan und seine Musik,* (Tutzing: Hans Schneider 1992)

Lander, N.S., The Recorder Homepage (research materials)
http://www.recorderhomepage.net/research.html

MacMillan, D., 'An Organological Overview of the Recorder 1800-1905', *Galpin Society Journal* LX 2007 pp191-202

Mahillon, V-C., *Catalogue descriptif et analytique de Musée Instrumental du Conservatoire Royal de Musique, Bruxelles* (Brussels : Les Amis de la Musique modern ed. 1973)

Meierott, L., *Die kleinen Flötentypen*, (Tutzing : Hans Schneider 1974)

Moeck, H., 'Csakane, Englische und Wiener Flageolette' in *Studia instrumentorum musicae popularis III,* (Stockholm: Nordiska Musikförlaget 1976)

Waterhouse, W., *The New Langwill Index*, (London: Tony Bingham 1993)

Young, P.T., *4900 Historical Woodwind Instruments*, (London: Tony Bingham 1993)

## THE RECORDER REVIVAL

Campbell, M., *Arnold Dolmetsch: the Man and his Work*, (London: Hamish Hamilton Ltd 1975)

Haskell, H., *The Early Music Revival – a History*, (London: Thames and Hudson Ltd 1988)

Hunt, E.H., *The Recorder and its Music*, (Hebden Bridge: Peacock Press Ltd 3rd ed. 2002)

Kirnbauer, M., 'Das war Pionierarbeit': die Bogenhauser Künstlerkapelle, ein frühes Ensemble alte Musik, in *Alte Musik – Konzert und Rezeption,* ed Gutmann, V., (Winterthur: Amadeus Verlag 1992)

MacMillan, D., 'Arnold Dolmetsch and the Recorder Revival', *The Consort* LXIII 2007 pp90-104

Thomson, J.M. (ed), *The Cambridge Companion to the Recorder,* (Cambridge: Cambridge University Press 1995)

Williams, A., 'The Dodo was really a Phoenix: the Renaissance and Revival of the Recorder in England 1879-1941' unpublished PhD diss. University of Melbourne 2005

# INDEX

American Civil War bands   129-130

Bavaria   102
Bellissent   34, 105, 106
Berchtesgaden   73, 102, 107, 110, 177
Berchtesgadner Fleitl   59-65, 85-86, 113-119
Berlioz, Hector   122
Bertani, Domenico   87
Billing, Friedrich   35
Boie, Johann Friedrich   88, 107
Bogenhauser Künstlerkapelle   39, 86, 170-172, 176
Bressan, Peter   148, 151
Bridge, Joseph Cox   124, 152
Burney, Charles   15, 40
Busby, Thomas   16

Camus   35
Chester recorders   124, 148, 149, 152, 153
Chouquet, G.   164
Church music   128-129
Colas, Prosper   36, 65, 102, 110
Constant, Pierre   166
Csakan   9-11, 118, 124, 133

Destuyver J.B.   89
Dolmetsch, Arnold   6, 111, 144, 147-152, 164, 176
Dolmetsch, Carl   6, 17, 22, 121, 153
Dupré, Pierre Paul Ghislain Joseph   36, 103, 105

Early Music Movement   143-145
Empfindsamkeit   19
Enlightenment, The   18
Engel, Carl   154
Exhibition of Instruments, South Kensington 1872   158
Exposition Universelle 1889   166
Exposition Universelle et Internationale 1890   167

Fétis, François-Joseph   173
Finn, A.J.   155
Firth, Pond & Co.   89, 107
Flageolet   11-13, 15, 87-89, 94, 123, 130, 133, 156, 161-163, 173
Flöten-schule und Ländler aus Berchtesgaden   118
Foot-joint   106

Galpin, Francis William   37-38, 90, 144, 156-158, 162, 176
Garsi   38
Gerlach, Gottlieb Johann   39
Goulding (firm of)   39-43, 90, 101
Gras, Charles   43
Grassi, Barnaba   83
Graz   102
Grenser, Heinrich   84

Hawkins, Sir John   16
Heberle, Anton,   10, 124
Hochschwarzer, A.   44

Iconography   133
Index of nineteenth-century recorders   26-34
Industrial Revolution   142
International Inventions Exhibition 1885   159
Ivry-la-Bataille   102, 168

Jacquot, A.   165
Jeantet, Jean   44, 105, 106

Keys on the recorder   105
Klein, Johann Joseph   127
Kleiner Tusch   121
Kruspe, Franz-Carl   45, 105, 106

La Couture-Boussey   59, 63, 101, 108, 166, 167-168
Lamy, Joseph Alfred   45, 101
Lansquenets, Band of   160
Lecomte, Arsène Zoë   46, 102
Linnell, John   135

*Index*

Literary references to the recorder  138
Löhner, Friedrich II  46
Löhner, Johann Andreas  47
Lot, Louis  91
Lot, Lucien  91

Macgregor, Malcolm  42, 97
Mahillon, Victor-Charles  48-53, 79-80, 109, 110, 111, 159-162, 173
Maker's marks  108
Martin, Jean-Baptiste  53
Martin, Johann Gottfried  54
Metzler, Valentine  6, 96
Music Loan Exhibition 1904  162

Noblet, F.  54, 169
Noblet et Thibouville  55

Oeggl, Bernardt  116
Oppenheim  55, 101

Paraffin Concerts  157-158
Parry, John  123
Patent voice flute  42, 97
Peter, Hildemarie  20
Peter Schmoll und seine Nachbar  121
Pitch marks  108
Pre-Raphaelites  133, 137
Prowo, Pierre  123

Recorder revival in Belgium  172-174
Recorder revival in England  147-164
Recorder revival in France  164-169
Recorder revival in Germany  170-172
Recorder revival in The Netherlands  174
Recorders in Norway  179
Romanticism  140
Royal Military Exhibition 1890  162
Rudall Carte  93, 155, 159

Sattler (family)   93
Schin   56
Schlosser (family)   179
Schubart, C.F.D.   15
Schulflöte   119
Schultze, Johann Christoph   123
Schweffer, Heinrich   56, 57
Shaw, George Bernard   160
Smart, George   94
Sonata Form   19
Sponge chamber   107
Sturm und Drang   19
Style galant   19
Swain, N.   126

Taffanel, Claude   166
Tans'ur, William   127
Tiersot, Julien   166
Thibouville-Cabart (firm)   57
Thibouville-Lamy (firm)   169
Tolbecque, August   99, 110
Townsend   58, 106, 108

Waitzman, Daniel   21-22
Walch, Lorenz I   85-86, 102, 113-115
Walch, Lorenz II   59-63, 102, 113-115, 117
Walch, Lorenz III   113-115
Walch, Paul   63-65, 102, 113-115, 117
Weber, Carl Maria von   121
Welch, Christopher   154
Woods (types)   107
Wrede, Hermann   94

*The Recorder In The Nineteenth Century*